PRAISE FOR *1 JOHN ON F.I.R.E.*

I have read a number of books on
vided the excellent job that Ken E
approach. This workable and pra
invaluable truths and wisdom. An
would do well to glean upon this
step-by-step study that will be a companion to the Bible for many years
to come.

REV. ROBERT W. RODGERS, EXECUTIVE DIRECTOR
NORTHWEST INDEPENDENT CHURCH EXTENSION

1 John on F.I.R.E. is a splendid combination of method and application.
Dr. Burge uses four basic principles (F.I.R.E.) to bring 1 John to life.
This innovative acronym can be used to study any book of the Bible,
bringing about new discoveries and personal challenges. I have used
F.I.R.E. with high school students and have seen its benefits through
practical application. This book lights up I John and gives you the tools
to illuminate the rest of God's Word.

NATHAN KEERAN, PRINCIPAL, BELAIR BAPTIST CHRISTIAN ACADEMY

For over thirty-two years, I've had the privilege to "sit under" the teaching
of Dr. Ken Burge, Sr. I'm excited that others outside of his immediate
church family now have the opportunity to learn how to study the Bible.
Using his F.I.R.E. technique, Ken has developed a unique Bible study
method that trains you, not only to accurately interpret the biblical text,
but also gives you his practical wisdom so you can put the text to work
in your daily life. Whether you are a Bible teacher, wife, mom, or layper-
son, *1 John on F.I.R.E.* will benefit your walk with the Lord.

KIMBERLY BURGE

1 John on Fire

1 JOHN

ON

F.I.R.E.

FAMILIARITY
INTERPRETATION
RELATIONSHIP &
EMPLOYMENT

Dr. Ken J. Burge, Sr.

ISBN-13: 9781940269580

Library of Congress: 2015950100

Cover design by Joe Bailen, Contajus Design

Printed in the United States of America

Contents

FOREWORD

I first met Ken, his wife, Kim, and their three boys, Joshua, Daniel, and Kenny, Jr. at an IFCA International convention in Orlando, Florida, in 1992. Ken and I developed a friendship over the last two decades while I was the president of Calvary Bible College and Seminary and now serving with Encouragement Ministries. It has been my privilege to preach at Ken's church, Colmar Manor Bible Church, and to stay in his home.

For over two decades I have followed the ministry of Dr. Ken J. Burge, Sr. His study of the biblical languages and extensive reading in related volumes has made him an articulate communicator and teacher. He has developed an effective ministry based on biblical exposition that leads to godly living.

Here, Dr. Burge has skillfully applied his F.I.R.E. method to 1 John. Bible students young and old would profit by employing the F.I.R.E. method of the author. His presentation is consistent throughout the book.

Utilized, the four steps make Bible study an adventure! *Familiarization*—reading carefully multiple times—prepares the heart and mind, and enables the reader to become a careful student in the process of interpreting and applying God's inspired Word. The author's method for *Interpretation* prevents spurious and careless handling of God's Word. Paul writes in 2 Timothy that the Word of God deals with the author's stated topic of *Relationships*, "thoroughly furnished unto all good works" (3:16, 17). This is an area of great profit. Dr. Burge's *Employment* of it is needed for the "so what" in all of Bible study.

Dr. Burge is to be commended for his consistency in using a style that will be a great help to many Bible students. His future volumes will also be welcomed additions to any personal library.

Dr. Elwood H. Chipchase
President, Encouragement Ministries
Former president, Calvary Bible College/Calvary Theological Seminary
Author of *Throughout the Years*

INTRODUCTION TO
1 JOHN ON F.I.R.E.

I grew up in a middle-class town that had tennis courts less than a quarter-mile from my home. As a youth, I could hop on my bicycle and literally coast downhill to my favorite location. My youthful dream consisted of winning at Wimbledon. The fact that I'm writing this commentary tells you that God took me down a different career path.

Being young had its advantages athletically; however, there were times that being young was a bummer. One warm evening a friend and I had patiently waited for a court to open. When players on the court (usually adults) went past their allotted time, it was customary to ask them if they'd be much longer. I did so to the couple playing on the nearest court—or at least making an honest attempt to play. The gentleman replied rather snidely, "Why don't you leave?" Clearly he'd misunderstood my question so I proffered it again, and he responded, "Soon."

Just as that novice tennis player didn't grasp the meaning of my polite question, I'm deeply concerned that many Christians don't understand the message of the Bible. Perhaps you are one of those well-meaning individuals who have tried repeatedly to comprehend the Word of God only to be frustrated again and again. If so, take heart, dear child of God: This book is designed with you in mind.

First John on F.I.R.E. is an inductive commentary. This simply means that instead of telling you what the Bible teaches, it takes you on the journey to discover its life-changing communication. My goal is that you not only learn how to derive the meaning of the biblical text before you, but also how to apply the message personally. In other words, my passion is to teach you how to develop the necessary skill set to become familiar with the Bible passage you are studying, interpret it accurately, relate it to its surrounding contexts, and employ it personally.

F.I.R.E. is the acronym used for our study. This mnemonic (memory) device stands for familiarity, interpretation, relationship, and employment.

We will use all four of these steps each time we travel through a section of Scripture together.

F represents familiarity. Although I've been privileged to study the Bible at both the undergraduate and graduate levels, the emphasis was always upon observation as the first step of Bible study. My friend, doesn't that term seem cold and clinical versus the warmness expressed by familiarity? The Word of God shouldn't be placed under the microscope and scrutinized by those wearing white coats in a sterile environment.

The origin of the word "familiarity" derives from the Latin *familiaritas* and means "familiar" or "intimate." Bible study should originate from a deep-seated personal relationship with God. *Familiarity* roars out intimacy and relationship with the living God while *observation* whimpers a frigid laboratory analysis of data.

Interpretation is the second stage of Bible study, represented here by the symbol **I**. Jesus has sent us a messenger to help us to understand the Scriptures—the eternal third member of the Godhead known as the Holy Spirit. Dependence upon Him is vital to enlighten our minds concerning God's truth. Jesus described the Holy Spirit as "the Spirit of truth" in John 16:13. He personally escorts us through the Bible, as the remainder of the verse says: "He will guide you into all truth."

Relationship becomes the third phase of our quest to understand the sacred text. The symbol **R** will stand for "relationship" throughout our travels. The Bible's value requires it to be treated with the utmost respect, "For the word of God is living and powerful, and sharper than any two-edged sword, piercing even to the division of soul and spirit, and of joints and marrow, and is a discerner of the thoughts and intents of the heart" (Heb. 4:12). We will see how the life-giving parts ally with the whole.

The fourth and final part of this most excellent adventure is employment, represented by the symbol **E**. Employment, or application, began when those who originally received the living Word were given their authoritative marching orders. We too will transition together, in order to determine not only how those to whom the Bible first came responded, but how we are called to respond today. God designed His Word to transform us into the image of Christ, and that cannot occur without our first personally employing the Bible to our lives.

Now that you've been given an introduction to the tools we'll be using, let's embark together upon the book of 1 John.

BACKGROUND

The author of 1 John doesn't identify himself in this five-chaptered epistle, yet early church tradition—including Irenaeus (130–212?), Clement of Alexandria (150–217), and Tertullian (160–220)—pegs the writer as the apostle John. Also, the Muratorian Canon (second century), which is the oldest existing list of New Testament books, cites John as the composer.

Unlike Paul, whose activities were often documented in the book of Acts, John's activities are not always known. Again, church tradition helps here and testifies to an elderly John writing this letter in the last part of the first century; the place of publication was perhaps Ephesus in Asia Minor (western Turkey).

John and his brother James were known as the sons of thunder (Mark 3:17). Early in Jesus' ministry they desired Him to call down fire on the Samaritans for not receiving Him (Luke 9:54). Jesus tamed this rabble-rouser into one who later would recline upon His breast at the Last Supper (John 13:23), and who would subsequently become known as the apostle of love.

The apostle's corralled fiery disposition would serve him well later in life, as he confronted three doctrinal heresies being propagated in Asia Minor. The first was an early form of Gnosticism, a movement which didn't become full-blown until the second century. The word "Gnosticism" derives from the word "knowledge." Gnostics held to dualism—a belief that held that spirit is good and matter is bad. In essence, the soul (immaterial) must be rescued from the body (physical). From this concept came the denial of Jesus having a physical body, which John vigorously refuted at the beginning of his epistle. Nine times in his letter, John gives tests for the believer to know what is true.

From this erroneous thought came Docetism and Cerinthianism. Docetism comes from a Greek word meaning "to seem." Docetists argued that Jesus' humanity was not real, but that He only appeared to have a human body. A proponent of this faulty system was Cerinthus, who believed that Jesus was the natural-born son of Joseph and Mary, and that after His baptism the Christ descended upon Him but departed prior to His crucifixion. Keeping in mind the false beliefs of Gnosticism, Docetism, and Cerinthianism will help you understand the erroneous doctrines that John confronted in his writings.

John's purpose in writing 1 John differs greatly from that of the gospel that bears his name. His stated intent of the gospel of John is in John 20:30-31: "And truly Jesus did many other signs in the presence of His disciples, which are not written in this book; but these are written that you may believe that Jesus is the Christ, the Son of God, and that believing you may have life in His name." The reason for writing his gospel was to display the deity of Jesus.

On the other hand, 1 John was written to confirm to believers their assurance of salvation through Jesus. "These things I have written to you who believe in the name of the Son of God, that you may know that you have eternal life, and that you may *continue to* believe in the name of the Son of God" (1 John 5:13).

First John can be divided into two parts. The *Reasons for Fellowship* comprises 1 John 1:1–2:27. John makes the case why believers should commune with the Father, Son, Holy Spirit, and other saints. Based upon those arguments comes the second half of 1 John, giving the *Reactions from Fellowship* in 1 John 2:28–5:21. Once we understand the *Reasons for Fellowship*, we should then have certain *Reactions from Fellowship*, as stated by John.

Now that the stage has been set, let's embark upon the gems that the Spirit of God gave to John to entrust to us.

PART ONE
REASONS FOR FELLOWSHIP

1 JOHN 1:1–2:27

CHAPTER ONE
JOHN, THE SENSIBLE APOSTLE

1 JOHN 1:1–4

—⁓⁓—

Three professionals were discussing their occupations and trying to prove why theirs was the oldest. There was a surgeon, an engineer, and a politician. The surgeon began the debate by saying, "I think the medical profession is the first line of work mentioned in the Bible. God made Eve by carving a rib out of Adam." Next the engineer offered, "No, engineering came first. Just think of the engineering job it took to create things out of chaos." The politician replied, "That's nothing. Who do you think *created* the chaos?"

One thing we know for sure is that God created people in order to have fellowship with them.

> That which was from the beginning, which we have heard, which we have seen with our eyes, which we have looked upon, and our hands have handled, concerning the Word of life—the life was manifested, and we have seen, and bear witness, and declare to you that eternal life which was with the Father and was manifested to us—that which we have seen and heard we declare to you, that you also may have fellowship with us; and truly our fellowship *is* with the Father and with His Son Jesus Christ. And these things we write to you that your joy may be full (1 John 1:1–4).

The Word that gives life
was from the beginning,
and this is the one
our message is about.
Our ears have heard,
our own eyes have seen,

and our hands touched
this Word.

The one who gives life appeared! We saw it happen, and we are witnesses to what we have seen. Now we are telling you about this eternal life
that was with the Father and appeared to us. We are telling you what we
have seen and heard, so that you may share in this life with us. And we share
in it with the Father and with his Son Jesus Christ. We are writing to tell
you these things, because this makes us truly happy (1 John 1:1–4, CEV).

WHY FELLOWSHIP MAKES GOOD SENSE—F

- Why does John begin his epistle by describing how he used his
  senses when encountering a physical and literal Jesus?
- What is the meaning of the expression "from the beginning" in 1
  John 1:1?
- Is it appropriate to use 1 John 1:2 as an argument for Jesus being
  God, since "that eternal life was with the Father?"
- What does the word "fellowship" mean in 1 John 1:3?
- How does 1 John 1:1-4 confront Gnosticism, Docetism, and
  Cerinthianism?

WHY FELLOWSHIP MAKES GOOD SENSE—I

John could be described as a sensible apostle. That is, he used his God-given
senses to verify that although Jesus was fully God, He also was fully man.
John's regular encounters with Jesus led to this eyewitness account of Jesus'
personhood. The firsthand information imparted from John to us refutes
the bad doctrine (propagated by Gnosticism, Docetism, and Cerinthianism)
that Jesus didn't have a literal body.

"That which" points to both Jesus' words and His personhood. After
all, He's called the "Word of life" at the end of the opening verse.

Next, John uses two perfect tense verbs to capture how he and the
apostles used two senses (hearing and seeing) to identify Jesus. The perfect

tense shows a completed action, but with the results continuing. John wrote about "that which was from the beginning, which we have heard, which we have seen with our eyes" in verse 1. In essence, John claims to have heard the very words of Jesus in the past and those words were still ringing in his ears; he also saw the Lord and could still envision Him as he wrote this epistle.

John's next statement is about his Savior, "which we have looked upon." We get our English word "theater" from the word used here. The apostle saw Jesus, if you will, on the big screen; he had the privilege to gaze attentively upon Him. Not only did John hear and see the Lord, he touched Him. He added, "and our hands have handled." Clearly Jesus wasn't a phantom; He had a physical body that could speak, be viewed from human eyes, and even be touched. John dispatched the erroneous views of Gnosticism, Docetism, and Cerinthianism with one fell swoop.

After verifying Jesus' humanity, John closes out verse 1, "concerning the Word of life." The clever apostle (or the Holy Spirit, without John understanding the broader meaning) gave another expression with a dual use. He deems Jesus as the incarnate (God made flesh) Word here in verse 1, but this assertion is also used elsewhere as a description of the heralding of the gospel. We will study this in more detail under Relationship.

Verse 2 states that "the life was manifested, and we have seen, and bear witness, and declare to you that eternal life which was with the Father and was manifested to us." "Manifested" means "to reveal openly." Jesus is a person and John restated from verse 1 for emphasis, "and we have seen" Him. He not only saw Jesus, but the present tense verb ("bear witness") shows that he continually gave testimony about Jesus. John's mission consisted of "declaring [another present tense verb] to you that eternal life." Cerinthus had denied the eternality of Jesus, but John declared that He "was with the Father and was manifested to us." Simply put, Jesus had been with God for all of eternity and then was *revealed openly* to the apostles.

John continues in verse 3, "that which we have seen and heard we declare to you." Once John referred to his apostolic sight and sound about Jesus, he gave the main verb, which controls the sentence, "we declare" to his audience.

He then stated his purpose, "that you also may have fellowship with us." The "you" is emphatic and stresses that the revelation of Jesus occurred so that Christians could have fellowship—a sharing in common—with one another. Our point of commonality is divine communion "with the Father and with His Son Jesus Christ."

Another purpose for writing to the saints is conveyed in verse 4, "that your joy may be full." Joy is a by-product of fellowship with the Father and Son, which fills the hearts of true believers. The apostle known for conveying God's love to the saints also desired his beloved children to experience the sublime joy of walking with God. Let's now transition to learn how 1 John 1:1–4 relates to the rest of this book and to the rest of the Bible.

WHY FELLOWSHIP MAKES GOOD SENSE—R

John began our epistle with, "That which was from the beginning." The phrase "from the beginning" occurs nine times in this book—in 1 John 1:1; 2:7 (twice), 13, 14, 24 (twice); 3:8, and 11. At times, these words seem to direct the readers to the beginning of the gospel proclamation they received. For instance, 1 John 2:7 states, "Brethren, I write no new commandment to you, but an old commandment which you have had from the beginning."

On other occasions, the focus seems to echo John 1:1, "In the beginning was the Word" which in turn connects to Genesis 1:1, "In the beginning God created the heavens and the earth." First John 2:13 appears to stress this, "I write to you fathers because you know Him *who* is from the beginning." I believe John, by direction of the Holy Spirit, was deliberately nonspecific in order to communicate both concepts. Therefore, "from the beginning" addresses both when those early disciples had heard the gospel, and also refers to Jesus who is eternally God. In essence, the One who became flesh was proclaimed by John ("from the beginning") and also pointed to Jesus being eternal ("from the beginning").

How fitting that John, the herald of the gospel, shared a message about the timeless Son of God who could be heard, seen, and felt. The phrase "the Word of life" doesn't just depict Jesus as the enduring Word, but is also used elsewhere as an assertion for the good news of the gospel. Observe that Paul encouraged the "holding fast the word of life" in Philippians 2:16, which captures this nuanced meaning.

Jesus' "life was manifested," according to 1 John 1:2. Paul marveled at this mystery in 1 Timothy 3:16, having written, "God was manifested in the flesh." The second member of the Godhead "which was with the Father" came to reveal the nature of the invisible God. Jesus petitioned the Father in John 17:5, "And now, O Father, glorify Me together with Yourself, with the glory which I had with You before the world was." John clearly showed both the humanity and deity of Jesus in 1 John 1:1–2.

John expressed his deep desire for the saints to have fellowship together, which also consisted of a personal relationship with both God the Father and God the Son. The triune God communes with believers. First John 1:3 shows that "truly our fellowship is with the Father." As early as Genesis 3:8 we see the Father having regular fellowship with Adam and Eve. Even after the merciful Father knew that Adam and Eve violated His law, He pursued them.

The Scripture clearly states that we also have communion with Jesus. First John 1:3 shares that, "truly our fellowship is with the Father and with His Son Jesus Christ." Paul informed the saints at Corinth, "God *is* faithful, by whom you were called into the fellowship of His Son, Jesus Christ our Lord" (1 Cor. 1:9). Does life get any better than sharing in a relationship with the maker of the heavens and earth, God, and our redeemer, Jesus Christ? And yet, there is more.

Second Corinthians 13:14 testifies to a three-fold fellowship with the Trinity. "The grace of the Lord Jesus Christ, and the love of God, and the communion [fellowship] of the Holy Spirit *be* with you all." The Father, who created the heavens and the earth (and you and me), with the Son, who laid down His life for us to be saved, and the indwelling Holy Spirit, all have entered into a personal relationship with the believer.

No wonder John could pen in 1 John 1:4, "And these things we write to you that your joy may be full." The apostle of love trumpeted the life-changing message of Jesus Christ; he had personally experienced the joy that Jesus talked about in John 15:11, and wanted his children in the faith to enjoy the same. Consider our beloved Lord's choice words in John 15:11 as we end this section: "These things I have spoken to you, that My joy may remain with you, and that your joy may be full."

WHY FELLOWSHIP MAKES GOOD SENSE—E

The way to derive an "employment point" consists of determining what action the author expected from his original audience. Once that is discovered, the application can be given in a modern setting. Since John writes to church-age saints, the correspondence between the initial recipients and the church today can readily be found.

Fellowship with God and believers for joyous living makes up our employment point. The purpose given for Jesus' manifestation and the apostle's declaration was "that you also may have fellowship with us; and truly our fellowship *is* with the Father and with His Son Jesus Christ" (1 John 1:3). This blissful communion with the saints, centered on the person of God, will subsequently produce joy. "And these things we write to you that [purpose] your joy may be full" (1 John 1:4). Putting these thoughts together gives us our application.

Specifically, here is what I want you to do: Develop a daily quiet time with God. This will be made up of reading God's Word and prayer. Our Lord has created us to commune with Him. On a personal note, I've been a believer for more than thirty-five years. The highlight of each day has been to meet with my Father, just as Adam and Eve met with Him (Gen. 3:8). Prioritize this now in your daily schedule and you won't be sorry.

Secondly, the Almighty has given us life and eternal life to not only meet with Him personally, but to worship and serve Him alongside other saints. The writer of Hebrews testifies to the need for believers to regularly assemble together: "Not forsaking the assembling of ourselves together, as *is* the manner of some, but exhorting *one another*, and so much the more as you see the Day approaching" (Heb. 10:25). We need each other to keep us focused on the day when Jesus will return.

If you don't have a church family, seek to find one immediately. Make sure that church has sound doctrine (right teaching that accurately reflects the message of the Bible). Ask the pastor for a copy of the church's constitution, which should include the doctrinal statement. (My advice if they don't have one: Run!) After you've been directed to a good church, make it a regular practice to attend faithfully. Then allow the Lord to lead you from there to a place of ministry in your church. Once you are daily fellowshipping with God and regularly worshiping and communing with other believers, you'll be firing on all cylinders spiritually—and God, through the Holy Spirit, will fill you with joy.

CHAPTER TWO

THE GOD OF LIGHT

1 JOHN 1:5–7

━━∿∿∿━━

An avid duck hunter was in the market for a new bird dog. His search ended when he found a dog that could actually walk on water to retrieve a duck. Shocked by his find, he was sure none of his friends would ever believe him. He invited a friend of his, a pessimist by nature, to hunt with him and his dog.

As they waited by the shore, a flock of ducks flew by. They fired, and a duck fell. The dog immediately jumped into the water. Amazingly, he didn't sink, but instead walked across the water to retrieve the bird, never getting more than his paws wet. The friend saw everything but didn't say a word. On the drive home, the hunter asked his friend, "Did you notice anything unusual about my new dog?" "I sure did," responded his friend. "He can't swim."

Some people just don't get the point. Let's carefully walk through the F.I.R.E. process again for 1 John 1:5–7, so together we can get the point.

> This is the message which we have heard from Him and declare to you, that God is light and in Him is no darkness at all. If we say that we have fellowship with Him, and walk in darkness, we lie and do not practice the truth. But if we walk in the light as He is in the light, we have fellowship with one another, and the blood of Jesus Christ His Son cleanses us from all sin (1 John 1:5–7).

> This is the message we have heard from him and declare to you: God is light in him there is no darkness at all. If we claim to have fellowship with him yet walk in the darkness, we lie and do not live by the truth. But if we walk in the light, as he is in the light,

we have fellowship with one another, and the blood of Jesus, his Son, purifies us from all (1 John 1:5–7, NIV)

THE PERKS OF LIGHT LIVING—F

- Who do the words "from Him" point to in 1 John 1:5?
- What does it mean that "God is light" in 1 John 1:5?
- Why does John use the words "if we say" in 1 John 1:6, 8, 10?
- If Jesus paid for all our past, present, and future sins when He died, why does the believer still need Jesus' blood to cleanse him from his sin (1 John 1:7)?

THE PERKS OF LIGHT LIVING—I

Who does John refer to when he says in 1 John 1:5, "This is the message which we have heard from Him?" Is the referent "from Him" pointing to the Father or the Son? Jesus is the nearest antecedent in verse 3. Moreover, He's the one of whom John said, "we have heard" back in verse 3. Jesus communicated to John, and then His beloved apostle shared that message to the saints at Ephesus and by way of extension, to us.

The apostle captures the true God's uncontaminated nature both positively and negatively in 1 John 1:5. First, he stated positively that, "God is light." This depiction from Jesus about the Father appears nowhere else in the Bible. Yet the Son came to reveal the essence of the invisible God to the world. The absolute purity of God was also revealed negatively by John's statement, "and in Him is no darkness at all."

John's word choice in 1 John 1:6, "If we say," (also in verses 8 and 10) seems to be directed at the false teachers who had infiltrated the church. They were inconsistent in their words and works. On the one hand they declare "that we have fellowship with Him" when referring to God, but really they "walk in darkness." The present tense use of "walk" shows that these idle talkers remained habitually in nightfall. That is, they were not saved.

Consider John as being from the "show-me state" of Missouri. He assessed the inconsistent pattern between the false brethren's speech and walk and said these individuals "do not practice the truth." Their denial of Jesus' humanity and deity classified them into the category of liars. Like oil and water, having fellowship with God and living in darkness don't mix.

These false teachers demonstrated by their lives that they were not in alignment with God. They walked in darkness (verse 6), and were neglecting the fellowship with the saints (verse 7). Since they were nonbelievers, they couldn't have true communion with the saints.

Conversely John wrote about Christians, "But if we walk in the light as He is in the light, we have fellowship with one another" (verse 7). As believers continually travel (as indicated by the present tense verb "walk") in God's light, they experience the pleasure of companionship with the body of Christ.

Walking in God's light has its continued benefits. John added, "and the blood of Jesus Christ His Son cleanses us from all sin." John does not hesitate to mention "the blood of Jesus Christ," showing that He was not a ghost or apparition but a real man, which contradicted Docetism. "Cleanses" is a present tense verb (used thirty times in the Greek New Testament), and since Christ's death happened decades earlier, it implies that it provided a removal of sins—past, present, and future. The power of the cross presently remains at work in the believer.

Finally, Jesus' shed blood cleanses the believer "from all sin." Notice that the word "sin" is singular. Christ's death has dealt with the *principle* of sin, not just its acts or effects. Let's now transition to gleaning an understanding of the implications of 1 John 1:5-7 from other parts of Scripture.

THE PERKS OF LIGHT LIVING—R

We are in the first major division of John, the *reasons for fellowship* (1:1–2:27). One of John's purposes why we should commune with the Lord and one another occurs in 1 John 1:5, "This is the message which we have heard from Him and declare to you, that God is light." Jesus came to reveal the attributes of the invisible Father; Jesus manifested openly the Father's light to the world. "No one has seen God at any time. The only begotten Son, who is in the bosom of the Father, He has declared Him" (John 1:18).

What does it mean, "that God is light?" Let me share some aspects of the light that might help us better comprehend the incomprehensible God. Jesus Himself announced, "I am the light of the world" in John 8:12. That "I am" is, in itself, a statement of deity (see Ex. 3:14; John 8:58). Jesus then added, "He who follows Me shall not walk in darkness, but have the light of life." God's luminosity accompanies salvation. Consider Psalm 27:1, "The LORD is my light and my salvation," wrote King David, "Whom shall I fear?"

God's light also incorporates His holiness. The psalmist describes the majestic God in Psalm 104:2 as follows: "Who cover *Yourself* with light as *with* a garment." Paul depicts the inaccessible radiance of God in 1 Timothy 6:16, "who alone has immortality, dwelling in unapproachable light, whom no man has seen or can see." This is why God told Moses, "For no man shall see Me, and live" in Exodus 33:20.

God's light encompasses His holiness and also purity. Enjoy James' character analysis of God's unimpeachable character: "Every good gift and every perfect gift is from above, and comes down from the Father of lights, with whom there is no variation or shadow of turning" (James 1:17). There exists no corruption or blemish in the Father of lights.

Let me point out just one more feature of God's marvelous light. Be astonished at Genesis 1:3 and what God effortlessly accomplished through His Word, "Let there be light; and there was light." He did this on day one of creation. However, it isn't until the fourth day that He created the sun and moon (Gen. 1:15–19). Where did the original light come from? God. Furthermore, the New Jerusalem to come will not need the sun and moon for light. Revelation 21:23 reports (emphasis added), "The city had no need of the sun or of the moon to shine in it, for the glory of God illuminated it. The Lamb *is* its light."

The children of God have been brought into the light; that's why it is incompatible for them to dwell in darkness. John showed this in 1 John 1:6, "If we say that we have fellowship with Him and walk in darkness, we lie and do not practice the truth." Paul shed light upon us on this very topic in 2 Corinthians 4:6, "For it is the God who commanded light to shine out of the darkness who has shone in our hearts to *give* the light of the knowledge of the glory of God in the face of Jesus Christ."

The benefits of remaining in God's light are stupendous. "But if we walk in the light as He is in the light, we have fellowship with one another, and the blood of Jesus Christ His Son cleanses us from all sin" (1 John 1:7). Psalm 119:105 states, "Your word *is* a lamp to my feet, and a light to my path." It is time again to allow the light of God's Word to give us our marching orders.

THE PERKS OF LIGHT LIVING—E

Live in God's light for fellowship and cleansing is our employment point this time. Please observe that this application point is phrased as an imperative. It is a command. The Lord never intended His children to sample God's Word without digesting it wholly. We do the joyous but arduous task of becoming familiar with the text, interpreting it accurately, relating it appropriately to its immediate and distant contexts, and then acting upon its message.

James conveys the importance of employing the Word of God. He astutely offered, "But be doers of the word, and not hearers only, deceiving yourselves. For if anyone is a hearer of the word and not a doer, he is like a man observing his natural face in a mirror; for he observes himself, goes away, and immediately forgets what kind of man he was. But he who looks into the perfect law of liberty and continues in it, and is not a forgetful hearer but a doer of the work, this one will be blessed in what he does" (James 1:22–25). God's blessing comes with the application of Scripture.

My friend, do you remember what it was like prior to putting your faith in Jesus, who died for your sin and was raised from the dead? Paul reminded those whom he had led to Christ at Ephesus, "For you were once darkness, but now *you are* light in the Lord. Walk as children of light" (Eph. 5:8). He had them recall that they were continually in darkness before coming to Christ—as shown by the imperfect tense "you were." Then he commanded them, "Walk as children of light." He then, like John, adds a negative command to the positive one: "And have no fellowship with the unfruitful works of darkness, but rather expose *them*. For it is shameful even to speak of those things which are done by them in secret" (Eph. 5:11-12). To remain in the light, one needs to shun the darkness.

In the previous chapter, I gave you marching orders to daily read your Bible, pray, and to start attending a church that is loyal to declare God's Word and to practice what it preaches. These are essential elements to stay in God's light, so that you can enjoy fellowship with God and likeminded Christians while experiencing cleansing. The living Word purifies the heart of the child of God. Paul referred to its inherent power in Ephesians 5:26 as "the washing of water by the word."

Dear friend, your next direct assignment is to memorize 1 John 1:7. The indwelling Holy Spirit will use the power of God's Word to keep you in the light, which will produce the benefits of fellowship, and the removal of filth.

Why add the memorization of biblical passages to one's daily habits? The answer appears in Psalm 119, the longest chapter of the Bible: "How can a young man cleanse his way? By taking heed according to Your word. With my whole heart I have sought You; Oh, let me not wander from Your commandments! Your word I have hidden in my heart, That I might not sin against You" (Ps. 119:9–11). Treasuring God's Word in your heart will keep you in the light.

Not only will memorizing God's Word guide you to paths of righteousness, but also it will enable you to challenge other believers to do the same. Consider Colossians 3:16, "Let the word of Christ dwell in you richly in all wisdom, teaching and admonishing one another in psalms and hymns and spiritual songs, singing with grace in your hearts to the Lord."

I know experientially that this newfound discipline of memorizing, and then meditating upon biblical passages, will richly enhance your walk with God. Remember, "But if we walk in the light as He is in the light, we have fellowship with one another, and the blood of Jesus Christ His Son cleanses us from all sin" (1 John 1:7).

CHAPTER THREE

CONFESSION IS GOOD FOR THE SOUL

1 JOHN 1:8–2:2

—≈≈≈—

I vividly recall an instance, now more than thirty-five-years ago, when I played the role of a knucklehead. (Shortly after this incident, I would come to Christ.) My friend had recently acquired his driver's license. There were a few of us cruising in his car drinking sodas, and we threw our bottles simultaneously out the window when we had finished our beverages. I remember hearing a loud smashing noise as the bottles hit the pavement. This mindless event occurred approximately one-half mile away from our destination (my friend's house).

Shortly after we reached our journey's end, I was in my buddy's back-yard when he called to me, saying there was a man at the front door with broken glass in his hands. Defiantly, I went to take out my knife because I didn't know what to expect when I reached the front of the house. As long as I live, I will never forget the admonition my friend gave me: "Kenny, put away the knife; it will just make him mad."

Have you ever wondered what a big, burly mountain man might look like? Well, I was about to see face to face the biggest and wildest looking man in my life. This incident always makes me remember Moe's quote from "The Three Stooges" when he observed a colossal figure of a man. He quipped, "That's not a man, that's a committee!" No wonder why my part-ner in stupidity said, "Kenny, put away the knife, it will just make him mad." Thankfully this gentle giant, who looked as big as King Kong, just gave us a much-needed lecture.

It wasn't long after this event that I was confronted with my sin as I was reading through the Bible for the first time, and started attending the church I now shepherd. The pastor's sermons were from the book of Romans. God's Spirit mightily used my personal Bible reading, coupled with the pastor's messages from Romans, to confront me about both my sin nature and practices of sin.

Conversely, the false teachers in 1 John 1:8, 10, denied both these things. Let's probe together what 1 John 1:8–2:2 has to say concerning sin and its manifestation. I can assure you that this text will, in return, probe your innermost thoughts and feelings as well.

> If we say that we have no sin, we deceive ourselves, and the truth is not in us. If we confess our sins, He is faithful and just to forgive us *our* sins and to cleanse us from all unrighteousness. If we say that we have not sinned, we make Him a liar, and His word is not in us.
>
> My little children, these things I write to you, so that you may not sin. And if anyone sins, we have an Advocate with the Father, Jesus Christ the righteous. And He Himself is the propitiation for our sins, and not for ours only but also for the whole world (1 John 1:8–2:2).

If we say that we have no sin, we deceive ourselves, and the truth is not in us. If we confess our sins, He is faithful and just to forgive us *our* sins and to cleanse us from all unrighteousness. If we say that we have not sinned, we make Him a liar, and His word is not in us.

My little children, these things I write to you, so that you may not sin. And if anyone sins, we have an Advocate with the Father, Jesus Christ the righteous. And He Himself is the propitiation for our sins, and not for ours only but also for the whole world (1 John 1:8–2:2, NASB).

CONFESSION IS SOULFULNESS AND SOUL FULLNESS—F

- What is the difference between, "If we say that we have no sin" (1 John 1:8), and "If we say that we have not sinned" (1 John 1:10)?
- What does the word "confess" mean in 1 John 1:9?

- How does Jesus fulfill the role of our Advocate in 1 John 2:1?
- Why does John use the present tense verb "is" concerning Jesus being "the propitiation for our sins" in 1 John 2:2?
- What is the meaning of the word "propitiation" in 1 John 2:2
- Did Jesus die for the whole world or just for those who would believe on Him?

CONFESSION IS SOULFULNESS AND SOUL FULLNESS—I

John exposed the misstatements of the false teachers introduced by the words, "If we say" in 1 John 1:6, 8, and 10. In verse 8 he boldly corrected the second fabrication of truth, "If we say that we have no sin, we deceive ourselves, and the truth is not in us." The Greek word for "sin" expresses "to miss the mark" and is singular; furthermore, it refers to the inherited principle of sin known as the sin nature. In other words: It's not just that we *do* sin, but that we were born *with* sin. It is our "nature."

First, the apostle flatly proclaims that if we deny having a sin nature, "we deceive ourselves." Moreover, this aberration shows that "the truth is not in us." To reject the clear and explicit biblical doctrine of inherited sin places the claimant at odds with God's revelation.

Some commentators believe that 1 John 1:9 was written for unbelievers to understand how to be saved. Yet this conflicts with John's stated purpose for writing this epistle (see 1 John 5:13); furthermore, salvation consists of more than just a confession of sin. The previous verse confronts those who deny having a sin nature. Therefore, in this verse, the apostle aims to communicate to the saints the importance of not denying inherited sin, and that confession, not denial of sin, is truly good for the soul.

The Greek term for "confess" denotes "to say the same thing." In other words, the penitent believer agrees with God that the embrace of a sinful thought or deed misses God's perfect standard and needs to be confessed. Observe how John transitions from the singular "sin" in verse 8 to the plural "sins" in verse 9. He lucidly makes the connection that sinful acts derive from a sinful nature, and need to be acknowledged to God as a violation of His absolute benchmarks.

John then points to God's attributes or perfections, to assure the believer that once confession was offered that He would grant forgiveness: "He is faithful and just to forgive us our sins and cleanse us from all unrighteous" (verse 9). "Faithful" refers to God's consistent character, and "just" reminds us that He always does what is right. He sends away (the literal meaning of "forgive") believers' sins once confession occurs.

Does John then return to the same thought of verse 8 in verse 10 when he writes, "If we say that we have not sinned, we make Him a liar, and His word is not in us"? I think not. Whereas verse 8 dealt with the sin nature, verse 10 pertains to sinful acts originating from the indwelling principle of sin passed down from Adam. The word "sinned" is in the perfect tense, showing a completed action, but with the results continuing. John teaches that if we claim not to have performed acts of sin, "we make Him a liar." Not only that, but "His word is not in us." To say that "we have not sinned" accuses God of being a liar and verifies that His Word, which declares that all people sin, doesn't abide within us.

Next, John appeals to the saints as to why they shouldn't capitulate to sin, and if they do, how they then should respond: "My little children, these things I write to you, that you may not sin. And if anyone sins, we have an Advocate with the Father, Jesus Christ the righteous" (1 John 2:1). John uses a term of affection by calling the saints "little children." The singular Greek word used here always occurs in the New Testament figuratively, referring to a teacher with his pupils.

John had a shepherd's heart and desired his flock not to sin. However, understanding the inherited principle of sin, and the acts that would follow, he wrote, "if anyone sins, we have an Advocate with the Father." Here Jesus, the Righteous One, becomes our Advocate. Once sin has been committed, it must be confessed to God, who alone can forgive based upon Jesus' shed blood for the believer.

Even now, "He Himself is [observe the present tense verb] the propitiation for our sins, and not for ours only but also for the whole world" (1 John 2:2). The noun "propitiation" occurs only twice in the New Testament, here and 1 John 4:10. Notice that Jesus isn't called the "Propitiator." This would suggest that He was like other high priests of the Old Testament who sprinkled blood on the mercy seat to cover sins. Conversely, Jesus Himself became our atoning sacrifice. He appeased the Father's wrath, by satisfying the demands of a holy God who cannot tolerate sin—by offering His own life as a sacrifice not only for believers, but for all of mankind.

These five verses are loaded with theological truths. Let's unpack them further in relationship.

CONFESSION IS SOULFULNESS AND SOUL FULLNESS—R

The Old Testament, like the New Testament, expresses the need for forgiveness. Proverbs 28:13 says, "He who covers his sins will not prosper, but whoever confesses and forsakes them will have mercy." First John 1:9 agrees: "If we confess our sins, He is faithful and just to forgive us our sins and cleanse us from all unrighteousness." Why then does a child of God have to confess his sins, if Jesus paid for all of them at Calvary? Shouldn't the need to confess sins be different after the cross, since, "He made Him who knew no sin *to be* sin for us, that we might become the righteousness of God in Him" (2 Cor. 5:21)? I'm glad you asked that question!

Think about your own family relationships as you view this text. It was my privilege to rear three sons (and please don't tell their mother I'm using her perfect angels in this illustration!). Imagine one of them does something wrong, like show disrespect toward me. Is the offender still my son? Absolutely! Yet, what will it take to have harmony in the Burge home again? The answer is confession. Once the child confesses to God and his dad that he's truly sorry for the act committed, the family unity—both heavenly and earthly—is firing again on all cylinders.

Yes, Jesus paid it all, and the application of His shed blood still applies today, as we learned from 1 John 1:7. However, in order to maintain the harmony between God the Father and His children, confession—agreeing with God that the act committed transgressed His Word—is needed in order to restore the family relationship to a right condition. This is also why confession is necessary for the child of God to keep himself right with his heavenly Father.

Speaking about Jesus' shed blood: For whom did Jesus die? There is a raging debate today on this most vital topic that addresses the very character of God. When Jesus was on the cross, He cried out, "It is finished" (John 19:30). The Greek word means "paid in full." Even at that time in history, this term was stamped on tax bills that had been paid. Does "paid in full" apply to everyone, or just to those who would believe in Jesus?

Dear brother or sister, look at how John described the sacrifice of Jesus in 1 John 2:2: "And He Himself is the propitiation for our sins, and not for ours only but also for the whole world." As has been stated long ago, when the plain sense of the text makes perfect sense, seek no other sense. John expressed that Jesus died not only "for our sins . . . but also for the whole world."

Let me phrase the debate another way: If God is love (and 1 John 4:8 says He is), could His Son die for just a percentage of people, and still be true to His nature? Jesus came "that whoever believes in Him should not perish, but have everlasting life" (John 3:16), since His death paved the way for everyone to be saved.

I love thinking about the marvelous character of our God. Let's move to employment, to see particularly what we should apply based upon this text.

CONFESSION IS SOULFULNESS AND SOUL FULLNESS—E

The purveyors of false doctrine denied both inherent sin and the manifestation of sin in their lives. John argued strongly against this erroneous doctrine, and in so doing gives us our first employment point: *Confess your sin and don't deny it* (1 John 1:8–10). From my opening illustration about the gentle giant, it's clear that I understood I was a sinner even before I came to Christ.

Even today, after having the privilege to walk with God for more than thirty-five years, I still know that I'm a sinner—now saved by grace. After studying Paul's epistles these many years, I might have one point of contention with him in heaven based upon 1 Timothy 1:15: "This *is* a faithful saying and worthy of all acceptance, that Christ Jesus came into the world to save sinners, of whom I am chief." Paul said this in his old age and used the present tense verb, showing how he viewed himself even in that season of life. If I were alive in Paul's day, I would have argued that he places second, right after me.

I've had the privilege to interact with many people about spiritual things over the last three decades, and to confront them about their lost condition. Honestly, I cannot recall one time when someone back-pedaled from being a sinner. I believe the reason for this has been a result of Jesus dispatching the Holy Spirit after He ascended to heaven. "And when He [the Holy Spirit] has come," Jesus declared, "He will convict the world of sin, and of righteousness, and of judgment" (John 16:8). The child of God should be quick to submit to the indwelling Spirit's conviction when he or she has sinned.

Your first assignment, then, consists of building a pattern of "short accounts." In other words, develop the habit of confessing your sin to God immediately after it occurs. God knows what you've done; confess your sin and don't cover up what's already known.

David, a man after God's own heart, learned the penalty for a prolonged unwillingness to confess his sins of adultery and murder concerning Bathsheba and Uriah the Hittite. Many scholars believe that Psalm 32 describes the account of David's affair with Bathsheba, and how God chastened him until he came clean. Consider the mighty warrior David who said, "When I kept silent, my bones grew old through my groaning all the day long. For day and night Your hand was heavy upon me; my vitality was turned into the drought of summer" (Ps. 32:3–4). And then, "I acknowledged my sin to You, and my iniquity I have not hidden. I said, 'I will confess my transgressions to the LORD.' And You forgave the iniquity of my sin" (Ps. 32:5). Don't wait; immediately confess any sin that the probing Holy Spirit brings to your mind from the past, and from this moment onward, keep short accounts.

Employment point number two piggybacks on the first one: *Consider your Advocate and don't sin* (1 John 2:1–2). Think about how God desires to keep you in the light. Moreover, ponder what it cost Jesus Christ, your Advocate, to wipe away your sin as far as the east is from the west.

Satan is the persistent "accuser of our brethren" (Rev. 12:10). He regularly hurls accusations to the Father about us, just as he did with Job.

Conversely, Jesus pleads our case to the Father. Even on earth, Jesus interceded for His own disciples. Our Lord went to bat for Peter and told him just before His arrest and crucifixion, "Simon, Simon! Indeed, Satan has asked for you ["you" is plural here, referring not only to Peter but the other apostles], that he may sift you as wheat. But I have prayed for you [singular here, indicating Peter], that your faith should not fail; and when you have returned to *Me*, strengthen your brethren" (Luke 22:31–32).

John penned his letter in part so that God's children would grasp how precious fellowship is and strive to please God always by not sinning. Indeed, we need to remember that Jesus suffered enormously both physically and spiritually before He took on the heavenly role as our Advocate. He experienced excruciating pain in conjunction with His death, and unmentionable emotional agony and distress displayed by pleading with His Father on the cross, "My God, My God, why have you forsaken Me?" (Matt. 27:46).

Jesus' death set us free from the bondage of sin. He resisted every temptation thrown at Him by the Devil. Because of this, we have a champion at the right hand of God. Turn to your Advocate in the moment of temptation, and bask in the liberty of not having to bow down to the lusts of the flesh, the lusts of the eyes, and pride of life. It's good to confess your sin once committed; it's better to rely upon Christ's power and resist it. As our beloved apostle earlier wrote, "And you shall know the truth, and the truth shall make you free" (John 8:32), and "Therefore if the Son makes you free, you shall be free indeed" (John 8:36).

CHAPTER FOUR

WE MUST WALK AS HE WALKED
1 JOHN 2:3–6

=~~~~~

Three friends decided to go deer hunting together: a lawyer, a doctor, and a preacher. As they were walking, along came a big buck. The three of them shot simultaneously. Immediately the buck dropped to the ground and all three rushed up to see how big it actually was. Upon reaching it they couldn't determine whose shot had actually killed the deer. A heated debate ensued, and a few minutes later a game officer came by and asked what the problem was. The doctor told him that they were debating who shot the buck. The officer took a look at the buck and within a few seconds, he said with much confidence, "The preacher shot the buck!" They all wondered how he knew that so quickly. The officer said, "Easy. The bullet went in one ear and out the other."

This preacher experientially understands that assessment! My prayer is that as we get familiar with 1 John 2:3–6, interpret it in light of its historical context, relate it to other appropriate Bible passages, we won't let it go in one ear and out the other.

> Now by this we know that we know Him, if we keep His commandments. He who says, "I know Him," and does not keep His commandments, is a liar, and the truth is not in him. But whoever keeps His word, truly the love of God is perfected in him. By this we know that we are in Him. He who says he abides in Him ought himself also to walk just as He walked (1 John 2:3–6).

> Now by this we know that we have come to know God: if we keep his commandments. The one who says "I have come to know God" and yet does not keep his commandments is a liar, and the

truth is not in such a person. But whoever obeys his word, truly in this person the love of God has been perfected. By this we know that we are in him. The one who says he resides in God ought himself to walk just as Jesus walked (1 John 2:3–6, NET).

WE MUST WALK THE JESUS WALK—F

- Do the pronouns "Him" and "His" in 1 John 2:3 point to the Father or the Son?
- Do "His commandments" in 1 John 2:3 refer to the Father or Son, and what are those commandments?
- Why is there a shift in 1 John 2:1–3 from the plural—"we have an Advocate" (verse 1), "our sins" (verse 2), "we know" (verse 3), "we keep" (verse 3)—to the singular "He who says," in 1 John 2:4?
- What does it mean that "the love of God is perfected" in the individual who "keeps his word" in 1 John 2:5?
- Who is the antecedent of "Him" and "He" in 1 John 2:6?

WE MUST WALK THE JESUS WALK—I

The repetition of the oft-repeated phrase in 1 John, "by this," introduces a test. (Many more examinations will follow throughout the book, led by these words.) John gave an objective means to gauge if believers truly know the Lord. "Now by this we know that we know Him, if we keep His commandments" (1 John 2:3). The nearest antecedent that seems to best fit the context to "Him" and "His" is Jesus, found in the previous verse. Therefore, we demonstrate that "we know Him [Jesus]" when "we keep His [Jesus'] commandments."

John used the same Greek word for "know" twice in this verse; it occurs 223 times in the New Testament and twenty-five times in 1 John. "Know" refers to experiential knowledge, and its first usage appears here in 1 John 2:3. It is used in the present tense, showing we continuously know Jesus if we meet the following condition: "we keep His commandments." Although the Gnostics claimed a superior knowledge of God,

John proclaims by the second use of "we know"—this time in the perfect tense—that we have come to know Jesus experientially in the past, and that the results continue for the believer, "if we keep His commandments." Obedience to God's Word produces a personal familiarity with the Holy One.

The apostle then moves from multiple verses (1 John 2:1–3) with the use of the first person plural ("we" and "our") to the use of the third person, "He who says" (1 John 2:4). Why? John includes himself in verses 1–3 as a genuine believer, but excludes himself in 2:4 because he's not an impostor. John exposes the duplicity of the unrighteous false teachers: "He who says, 'I know Him,' and does not keep His commandments, is a liar, and the truth is not in him" (1 John 2:4). Here John chooses the perfect tense, announcing that these liars have never known the Lord in the past and don't experience Him now.

By contrast, John wrote, "But whoever keeps His word, truly the love of God is perfected in him. By this we know that we are in Him" (1 John 2:5). John seems to use "His word" as a synonym for "His commandments" in verses 3 and 4. Could John have written verse 5 to refute the false teachers who perhaps were claiming to exclusively know God? One thing is for sure: God's "perfected" (perfect tense) love shows that the obedient Christian's love *has been made complete* or *mature* in the past and continues presently. The last part of verse 5, "By this we know [again, an experiential knowledge] that we are in Him" reveals the results of standing complete in God's perfected love and builds a bridge to verse 6.

John reveals the fallacy of the false teachers who claim to have a close walk with God: "He who says he abides in Him ought himself also to walk just as He walked" (1 John 2:6). The present tense of "abides" communicates that the false teachers proclaimed that they regularly walked with God. John exposed their inconsistency because they said one thing and did another. "Ought" speaks of obligation; those who truly know God model their relationship with Him by walking as Jesus did. Imitation truly becomes the highest form of flattery for the child of God, who resides in God by walking with Jesus.

This short passage of Scriptures exudes a broader relationship than that given in these four verses. Let's move on to consider how 1 John 2:3–6 relates more expansively in the Bible.

WE MUST WALK THE JESUS WALK—R

Knowing God personally permeates this book. Now for the first time, we're introduced to the verb "know" in 1 John 2:3. The benefits of knowing God personally and experientially transcend mere head knowledge because the Lord lives in us. Paul expressed this beautifully in Colossians 1:27, "Christ in you, the hope of glory."

Our word has a rich etymology. It can be found in the Greek translation of the Old Testament (called the Septuagint, or LXX) in the book of beginnings known as Genesis. From Genesis 4:1 we see how this knowledge goes beyond just comprehension of information. "Now Adam knew Eve his wife, and she conceived and bore Cain." The first man's sexual relationship with his rib-built wife reveals the experiential knowledge as translated by "knew."

By the same token, the apostle Paul's longing to fellowship with Jesus comes through passionately in Philippians 3:8, "But indeed I also count all things loss for the excellence of the [experiential] knowledge of Christ Jesus my Lord, for whom I have suffered the loss of all things, and count them as rubbish, that I may gain Christ." Some scholars relate the word "rubbish" to the idea of something thrown to the dogs and refers to that which is worthless while others tie it to the word "dung." Paul considered whatever he sacrificed to know Jesus experientially as table scraps or refuse. Moving forward two verses, Paul wrote, "that I may know Him [Jesus as mentioned in verse 8] and the power of His resurrection, and the fellowship of His sufferings, being conformed to His death" (Phil. 3:10). Both John and Paul had this in common: They had a deep desire to have an experiential knowledge of Jesus, and for God's children to want that also.

To know God at this level can only happen "if we keep His commandments" (1 John 2:3). Jesus laid out the church's charge known as the Great Commission in Matthew 28:18–20: "All authority has been given to Me in heaven and on earth. Go therefore and make disciples of all the nations, baptizing them in the name of the Father and of the Son and of the Holy

Spirit, teaching them to observe all things that I have commanded you; and lo, I am with you always, *even* to the end of the age." The main verb here is "make [disciples]" and is accompanied by three participles, "go," "baptize," and "teach." Notice that Jesus said in verse 20 "to observe all things that I have commanded you." The obedience to all that Jesus commanded will produce an experiential knowledge of Him.

For more than three years, our Lord Jesus modeled to His disciples how to live. Just before His death for them and all people, He desired to communicate that they needed to be willing to also lay down their lives for one another. After washing their feet by taking on the role of a slave, He said, "For I have given you an example, that you should do as I have done to you. Most assuredly, I say to you, a servant is not greater than his master; nor is he who is sent greater than he who sent him. If you know these things, happy are you if you do them" (John 13:15–17). The application of Jesus' commandments will produce a joyful experiential knowledge.

Knowledge is a wonderful thing if it is applied. Press on, my dear friend, and commit to do what lies before you.

WE MUST WALK THE JESUS WALK—E

Practice God's individual commandments to display you know Him becomes our first employment point, based upon 1 John 2:3–4. To "keep His commandments" (1 John 2:3) carries the idea to watch over or guard those commandments.

Israel's first king failed to honor God's Word. On two separate occasions (1 Sam. 13, 15), Saul didn't obey the specific commands given to him. In the first instance, he offered a priestly sacrifice when he didn't have that authority (1 Sam. 13:5–9). Then the disobedient king only partially fulfilled obliterating the Amalekites and all their livestock (1 Sam. 15:7–9). Read carefully Samuel's summation of these matters in 1 Samuel 15:22–23: "Has the LORD as *great* delight in burnt offerings and sacrifices, as in obeying the voice of the LORD? Behold, to obey is better than sacrifice, and to heed than the fat of rams. For rebellion *is as* the sin of witchcraft, and stubbornness *is as* iniquity and idolatry. Because you have rejected the word of the

LORD, He also has rejected you from being king."

David, who was called "a man after His [God's] own heart" (1 Sam. 13:14), was on a different spiritual place from the previous king. What set the two apart? David willingly and wholeheartedly did all of God's bidding, while Saul picked and chose what he'd do. Dear brother or sister, commit right now to becoming a David. Bow your head and tell the Lord that you will *practice God's individual commandments to display you know Him.*

Our second application point closely resembles the first one but with a slight change: *Practice God's entire Word to display that you love Him* (1 John 2:5). Let's review 1 John 2:5 again, "But whoever keeps His word, truly the love of God is perfected in him." We should not only show the world that we know God by our obedience to His individual commandments, but also model that we love Him by our total allegiance.

Abraham is called the father of faith. Romans 4:20 says, "He did not waver at the promise of God through unbelief, but was strengthened in faith, giving glory to God." However, when did this great patriarch (who, by the way, had his struggles—see Genesis 12–21) receive the recognition of heaven that he loved God? It came after he was willing to sacrifice his son Isaac—his supreme test. Genesis 22:12 reports the angel of the Lord's announcement to Abraham, "Do not lay your hand on the lad, or do anything to him; for now I know that you fear God, since you have not withheld your son, your only *son*, from me." Right now, again bow your head and inform the Lord of your intention that you will *practice God's entire Word to display that you love Him.*

Our third and final employment is: *Reside with Jesus to display your relationship with God.* It is time for you to determine to do the Jesus walk. "He who says he abides in Him ought also to walk just as He walked" (1 John 2:6). Jesus' life is beautifully displayed for us in detail in the gospels and many applications of His words are given in the epistles. Know His commandments and obey them.

The Christian journey isn't easy. The Christian life should be viewed as a battleground and not a playground. Jesus suffered much; all who do the Jesus walk will also experience difficulties through trials and persecution. Yet Peter wrote, "For to this you were called, because Christ also suffered for us, leaving us an example that you should follow His steps" (1 Pet. 2:21). My sincere prayer for all of you who study 1 John through this inductive commentary is that you will learn much and put that learning "into shoe leather."

CHAPTER FIVE

SOMETHING OLD, SOMETHING NEW

1 JOHN 2:7–11

———≈∿∿≈———

A pastor was on vacation, so he let his assistant pastor preach in his absence. When the pastor returned from vacation, he saw one of the church members and asked him how the assistant preacher did. The man said that it was a poor sermon that lacked substance. Shortly thereafter, the pastor saw the assistant pastor and asked him how the sermon went on Sunday morning. The assistant replied, "Excellent! I didn't have time to prepare anything myself, so I preached one of your sermons."

Unlike the assistant pastor's sermon, which consisted of something old and something new but still lacked substance, 1 John 2:7–11 exudes meaningfulness. Let's carefully and prayerfully read the inspired Word of God:

> Brethren, I write no new commandment to you, but an old commandment which you have had from the beginning. The old commandment is the word which you heard from the beginning. Again, a new commandment I write to you, which thing is true in Him and in you, because the darkness is passing away, and the true light is already shining.
>
> He who says he is in the light, and hates his brother, is in darkness until now. He who loves his brother abides in the light, and there is no cause for stumbling in him. But he who hates his brother is in darkness and walks in darkness, and does not know where he is going, because the darkness has blinded his eyes (1 John 2:7–11).

My dear friends, I am not writing to give you a new commandment. It is the same one that you were first given, and it is the message you heard. But it really is a new commandment, and you know its true meaning, just as Christ does. You can see the darkness fading away and the true light already shining.

If we claim to be in the light and hate someone, we are still in the dark. But if we love others, we are in the light, and we don't cause problems for them. If we hate others, we are living and walking in the dark. We don't know where we are going, because we can't see in the dark (1 John 2:7–11, CEV).

THE CONTINUITY OF THE OLD AND NEW—F

- What is the "old commandment" mentioned in 1 John 2:7?
- What is the "new commandment" referred to in 1 John 2:8?
- Who is he who "hates his brother" in 1 John 2:9?
- Why doesn't John say "he who says" in 1 John 2:10, as he did in 1 John 2:9?
- Why is "there no cause of stumbling" for the one "who loves his brother" in 1 John 2:10?

THE CONTINUITY OF THE OLD AND NEW—I

For the first time in this epistle, John addressed the saints as "brethren." Although the word appears seventeen times in 1 John, both times that it is used as a direct address known as a vocative—here, and again in 1 John 3:13—it occurs in the context of loving the brethren. John then adds, "I write no new commandment to you" (1 John 2:7). The word used for "new" emphasizes quality. John's word choice showed that this wasn't a newly introduced commandment.

The fatherly apostle continued to write in verse 7 that it is "an old commandment which you have had from the beginning." He then closes out verse 7 with, "The old commandment is the word which you heard from the beginning." Decades earlier, Jesus had commanded His followers to love one another. *That* is the old commandment from the standpoint of John's audience, since Jesus spoke it many years ago.

The apostle then masterfully and creatively continues his line of thinking in 1 John 2:8, "Again, a new commandment I write to you," which seemingly contradicts verse 7. How can it be both old and new? Again, John emphasizes that it is new in quality. It became a "new commandment" to John's readers, since they had received the commandment to love from John personally and not Jesus. They will now directly experience it for themselves.

Jesus had genuinely practiced the Old Testament commandment to love one's neighbor (and did the same for His enemies) in a new or fresh way. That is why John could write, "which thing [pointing to the newness of the commandment and not the commandment itself] is true in Him [Jesus] and in you." How marvelous that John's spiritual children had the occasion to practice loving one another anew, as did Jesus to His generation.

John then adds, "because the darkness is passing away, and the true light is already shining." Believers experience victory over sin because the One who kept the commandments in a new and living way is also the light of the world. His light now shines through us and will continue to do so until He returns.

John now introduces another fatal flaw of the false teachers in 1 John 2:9: "He who says he is in the light, and hates his brother, is in darkness until now." The word "hates" here occurs in the present tense and testifies to the group of false instructors who are characterized by their lack of love toward the saints. These fraudulent imitators are "in the darkness until now." Even as John penned this account, the purveyors of animosity still remained in the gloominess of their sin.

The apostle equates love with action in 1 John 2:10, "He who loves his brother abides in the light, and there is no cause of stumbling in him." The verb for "love" speaks of the highest kind of love directed from the will, and appears in the present tense. John stated positively that the believer who loves regularly resides in God's luminescence and therefore won't trip up his brother by his activities, since the Lord governs them. Abiding in the light keeps the child of God from both stumbling and from being a stumbling block to others.

John then states the concept negatively in 1 John 2:11, "But he who hates his brother is in darkness and walks in darkness, and does not know where he is going, because the darkness has blinded his eyes." In other words, the one who continually hates lives under the dominion of Satan and remains without God's light because the prince of darkness "has blinded his eyes." John shows a stark contrast between the children of light (genuine believers) and the children of darkness (false teachers) in 1 John 2:7–11. We will now further explore these opposites, under relationship.

THE CONTINUITY OF THE OLD AND NEW—R

Jesus' teachings surpassed the commandment from Leviticus 19:18 "to love your neighbor as yourself." In the Sermon on the Mount, He stated, "You have heard that it was said, 'You shall love your neighbor and hate your enemy.' But I say to you, love your enemies, bless those who curse you, do good to those who hate you, and pray for those who spitefully use you and persecute you" (Matt. 5:43–44).

John picks up on Jesus' prior teaching: "Brethren, I write no new commandment to you, but an old commandment which you have had from the beginning. The old commandment is the word which you heard from the beginning" (1 John 2:7). The old commandment from John's current ministry was a new commandment from Jesus perhaps fifty years prior: "A new commandment I give to you, that you love one another; as I have loved you, that you also love one another" (John 13:34).

What did John mean in 1 John 2:7 when he wrote, "the old commandment is the word which you heard from the beginning? The "word" refers to Jesus' message that He spoke often. Carefully consider Jesus' instructions to His disciples shortly before His death: "This is My commandment, that you love one another as I have loved you. Greater love has no one than this, than to lay down one's life for his friends" (John 15:12-13). Jesus practiced what He preached; within the next twenty-four hours He would lay down His life for *His* friends—us.

Jesus' directives become fresh or new to every generation of believers. John would tell his beloved children, "By this we know love, because He laid down His life for us. And we also ought to lay down *our* lives for the brethren" (1 John 3:16). But how should subsequent generations from Jesus, who might not have to literally die for another, act? Hence we have 1 John 3:17–18, "But whoever has this world's goods, and sees his brother in need, and shuts up his heart from him, how does the love of God abide in him? My little children, let us not love in word or in tongue, but in deed and in truth." The answer lies in showing the same compassion Jesus extended to His brethren, through sacrificially meeting one another's needs.

Now that we have a better understanding of something old and something new, let's see how this should be acted upon.

THE CONTINUITY OF THE OLD AND NEW—E

No one has ever loved to the extent that Jesus did. He becomes our pattern for caring for the saints. At the beginning of the chapter where Jesus washed the disciples' feet, we have the following introduction, "Now before the feast of the Passover, when Jesus knew that His hour had come that He should depart from this world to the Father, having loved His own who were in the world, He loved them to the end" (John 13:1). "He loved them to the end" conveys that He loved His disciples with all of His being. What a beautiful model for us to imitate.

Now let's observe the employment point derived from the inspired instruction of the apostle of love in 1 John 2:7–11: *Demonstrate your love for God by loving the brethren.* Whereas the children of darkness and the false teachers demonstrated their soiled hearts by hating the brethren, we are to reflect God's love in our lives by tending to the needs of our brothers and sisters.

Paul also addressed the extension of benevolence at the appropriate time to mankind in general but to Christians in particular in Galatians 6:10, "Therefore, as we have opportunity, let us do good to all, especially to those who are of the household of faith."

God has a sense of humor and timing. As I was praying about how to write this final part of the chapter, my telephone rang. It was Margo, my daughter-in-law, who had water coming into her basement after two days of heavy rain. "Opportunity" from Galatians 6:10 literally means "season." Think rainy season here! After my delay from mopping a wet basement—not the most glorious project ever—I'm back to my closure of this chapter with the practical application God gave me.

My dear friends, when you *demonstrate your love for God by loving the brethren*, it isn't always timely or even necessarily sanitary. Yet as the Father orchestrates opportunities for service, you are showing your brothers and sisters in Christ, God's love. I must confess I had a silent but smiling cheerleader helping me to enjoy my task. My two-month-old granddaughter Kylee Joy was propped up in a clothesbasket, and smiled and cooed as I worked. Not bad—a gorgeous non-verbal cheerleader at my side for earth's toils, and the Father's gracious reward awaiting me in heaven.

Mop on for Jesus to *demonstrate your love for God by loving the brethren*.

CHAPTER SIX

IT IS TIME FOR A SPIRITUAL CHECK-UP

1 JOHN 2:12–14

———≈∧∧∿∿———

Two hunters flew deep into the remote backwoods of Canada to hunt elk. They bagged six elk. The pilot told them that the plane could only carry four of the elk out. The hunters protested, "But the plane that carried us out last year was exactly like this one. The horsepower was the same, the weather was similar, and we had six elk then."

Hearing this, the pilot reluctantly agreed to try. They loaded the six elk and took off, but sure enough, there was insufficient power to climb out of the valley with all that weight, and they crashed.

As they stumbled from the wreckage, one hunter asked the other if he knew where they were. "Well, I'm not sure," replied the second hunter, "but I think we are about two miles from where we crashed last year."

How far have you gone spiritually in the last year, my dear friend? Have you grown, or have you crashed? It is time for a spiritual check-up from 1 John 2:12–14:

> I write to you, little children,
>> Because your sins are forgiven you for His name's sake.
> I write to you, fathers,
>> Because you have known Him *who is* from the beginning.
> I write to you, young men,
>> Because you have overcome the wicked one.
> I write to you, little children,
>> Because you have known the Father.
> I have written to you, fathers,

Because you have known Him *who is* from the beginning.
I have written to you, young men,
Because you are strong, and the word of God abides in you,
And you have overcome the wicked one (1 John 2:12–14).

I write to you, dear children, because your sins have been forgiven on account of his name. I write to you, fathers, because you have known him who is from the beginning. I write to you, young men, because you have overcome the evil one. I write to you, dear children, because you have known the Father. I write to you, fathers, because you have known him who is from the beginning. I write to you, young men, because you are strong, and the word of God lives in you, and you have overcome the evil one. (1 John 2:12–14, NIV 84)

PURSUING SPIRITUAL ADULTHOOD—F

- Is John addressing different age groups or different maturity levels in 1 John 2:12-14?
- Why does John add a "because" to every "I write" section in this passage? What do all three groups have in common?
- Who are the "little children" in 1 John 2:12? How are they distinct from the "little children" of verse 13?
- Who are the "fathers," "young men," and "little children" in 1 John 2:13?
- Why does John only repeat the fathers and young men and not the little children in 1 John 2:14?

PURSUING SPIRITUAL ADULTHOOD—I

How should we interpret the text before us? Some believe that John addresses all Christians as fathers, young men, and little children. If that's the case, why then does John address them separately? Others see John pointing to different age groups within the church. Yet does age necessarily reflect spiritual maturity? The passage seems best to me to be understood as John targeting three separate groups at different levels of spiritual maturity.

John began our portion of Scripture by communicating to the entire congregation. He penned, "I write to you, little children." The Greek word John used literally translates to "born ones." (This same term occurs also in 2:1, 28; 3:7, 18; 4:4; and 5:21.) Here, John is contrasting true believers from the false.

After each of the six uses in 1 John 2:12–14 of the various forms of "I write," John follows the expression with the word "because." In 1 John 2:12, after writing to the whole church, he gives the cause for the address, "Because your sins are forgiven you for His name's sake." All three groups of believers have had their sins dispatched, or sent away, by the name that is above every name, Jesus.

The apostle targeted the group that he belonged to first. "I write to you, fathers." They are the mature saints in the church, whether men or women. The reason for their full-grown spiritual status is then given: "because you have known Him who is from the beginning" (1 John 2:13). We've seen the term for "have known" earlier in this epistle and it means "to know experientially." John uses the perfect tense verb to show that these fathers have known Jesus personally in the past, and that the relationship continues. Seasoned believers are produced through many years of a consistent walk with the eternal Lord, "who is from the beginning."

Moving on, John engages the "young men." The Greek word for "young men" refers to that which is new or young, and speaks of a man in the prime of his invigorated life. Although not old enough to have gleaned the title of "fathers," they have done battle with Satan and have known victory. John stated the cause of their triumph, "Because you have overcome the wicked one." The verb for "overcome" conveys that these maturing believers have prevailed over Satan in the past, and continue to do so.

John then transitions to the "little children." This is a different Greek word than the one that appears in 1 John 2:12. It speaks of a child under the care and discipline of others. Perhaps as new converts (or those who haven't grown spiritually as they ought), they received the reason for their status, "Because you have known the Father." Nothing more is stated, other than they have a personal relationship with God.

To finish out the paragraph, John uses a literary device known as an epistolary aorist. An epistolary aorist conveys that John, the writer, understood the letter from the vantage point as already being in the hands of his readers. This explains the past tense use of "I have written." He then focuses upon the two upper tier groups, "I have written to you fathers, because you have known Him who is from the beginning. I have written [another epistolary aorist] to you, young men, because you are strong, and the word of God abides in you, and you have overcome the wicked one" (1 John 2:14).

Let's unpack the meaning of 1 John 2:14. John stressed why the fathers had that appellation, "Because you have known Him *who is* from the beginning." Again, the perfect tense verb declares that these mature saints have had longevity in their walk with God and continue in that practice.

Although John described the fathers in the same way, he adds an element about the young men. He cited that the reason for their position was "Because you are strong, and the word of God abides in you." The present tense verb "abides" speaks to the enduring influence that the indwelling Word has upon the child of God. This powerful entity enabled these maturing Christians to "overcome the wicked one."

Did you notice which group doesn't get mentioned again at the end of 1 John 2:14? The "little children" of verse 13 aren't addressed a second time like the "young men" and "fathers." Why? John didn't want anyone to remain in that category. His pastoral heart longed for all the children of God to press on to the status of "young men" and eventually "fathers."

I can't wait to show you how these three groups can better be understood in relationship to the rest of Scripture.

PURSUING SPIRITUAL ADULTHOOD—R

To pursue spiritual adulthood, one must be born again. John affectionately called the saints at Ephesus "little children" in 1 John 2:12. Whether he subsequently addresses fathers, young men, or little children, they are all believers.

Conversely, when the apostle Paul confronted the Corinthians about their carnality, he introduced that section of Scripture showing the saints of Corinth a portrait of the unsaved. He wrote, "But the natural man does not receive the things of the Spirit of God, for they are foolishness to him; nor can he know *them*, because they are spiritually discerned" (1 Cor. 2:14). The "natural man" literally is the "soulish man" who doesn't receive (literally, "welcome"), the Lord nor His Word. They grope about this world in spiritual darkness.

John begins his assessment of the spirituality of believers with the term "fathers." The implication of this word communicates maturation. Again, I believe Paul also captures the idea behind this term in 1 Corinthians 2:15: "But he who is spiritual judges all things, yet he himself is *rightly* judged by no one." The truly full-grown saint has learned to appraise everything by the Word of God; this description fits the man or woman who has faithfully practiced this trait over an extended period of time.

Next come the "young men." They haven't lived long enough to be classified as fathers, but demonstrate regular victory over sin in their lives as a result of having God's Word stationed internally. These rapidly growing saints have consistently lived up to Paul's admonition to Timothy in 1 Timothy 4:12, "Let no one despise your youth, but be an example to the believers in word, in conduct, in love, in spirit, in faith, in purity." Moreover, these young people grasp the wisdom of Paul in 1 Corinthians 15:33, "Do not be deceived, 'Evil company corrupts good habits.'"

Lots of young adults (and not-so-young adults) have a pair of Nikes in their closets. The Greek term *nike* means "conquest" or "victory." The verbal form of *nike* appears in 1 John 2:12, when John penned to the young men, "And you have overcome [*nike*] the wicked one." Maturing believers know what to run from—and to whom to run. Consider 2 Timothy 2:22, "Flee also youthful lusts; but pursue righteousness, faith, love, peace with those who call on the Lord out of a pure heart." In essence, "young men" are fugitives from impure desires, and choose to run tgrowing Christians with similar virtues.

Finally, John spoke to the "little children" in 1 John 2:13. The apostle simply stated about them, "Because you have known the Father." This group most likely consisted of those who recently got saved and didn't have the time to yet advance toward the listing of "fathers" or "young men." In all likelihood, "little children" also comprised those saints who have been saved long enough to step into the ranks of the maturing ("young men" and "fathers"), but haven't applied God's Word as those two groups had.

Paul classified this segment of the latter subset (the carnal) in 1 Corinthians 3. Clearly Paul was speaking about saved people in 1 Corinthians 3:1–3 because he called them "brethren" in verse 1: "And I brethren, could not speak to you as to spiritual *people* but as to carnal, as to babes in Christ. I fed you with milk and not with solid food; for until now you were not able to *receive it*, and even now you are still not able; for you are still carnal. For where *there are* envy, strife, and divisions among you, are you not carnal and behaving like *mere* men?"

Did you catch Paul's equation between the "carnal" and being "babes in Christ?" My pastoral heart breaks over those who should long ago have advanced in their Christian life to support the work of ministry, but rather have sown discord in the church through their childish ways.

Now that we've evaluated fathers, young men, and little children from other portions of Scripture, it is time to employ our primary passage.

PURSUING SPIRITUAL ADULTHOOD—E

The two hunters introduced at the beginning of our chapter had one thing going for them: They measured their progress over the course of a year. How about you, my dear brother or sister? When was the last time you took a spiritual inventory of your life? John certainly didn't write this paragraph for a purely informational purpose. I believe his main objective in penning this passage, which will be our employment point, consists of: *Evaluate your maturity and seek adulthood.*

Your assignment begins with an honest self-assessment of your spiritual standing before God. First, determine if you are truly a child of God. Have you placed your faith in Jesus who died for your sin and rose from the dead (demonstrating His victorious power over the grave)? Please take a moment right now if you've never believed in Jesus, and bow your head telling Him what He already knows: that you are a sinner. Furthermore, from the depth of your heart let Him know that you are trusting Him right now as the substitute for your sin, and that you're receiving the free gift of eternal life based upon His perfectly lived life that culminated in His death and resurrection for you.

If you've just trusted in Christ alone for salvation, welcome to the family. Turn to and read 1 John 5:13, and receive the assurance that you have the gift of life and are eternally secure.

Perhaps you've come to the conclusion that you are a child of God but haven't grown spiritually, whether due to a lack of time (you were recently saved), or because of carnal practices. Therefore you would place yourself in the category of "little children." Just as the Lord designed small children to develop physically, He longs for you to grow spiritually. Would you commit right now to strive to become a "young man" with the intent of being a "father" one day? This journey begins with a daily commitment to read and apply God's Word to your life, and to cultivate a prayer life showing dependence on the Almighty. I commend those of you who've just made this Lord-honoring goal your own.

Moving on to the ultimate goal—spiritual fatherhood—let me share my reflections on the American church today. One of the observations that I have is that we're grossly understocked with mature men and women who fit the bill of "fathers." It seems much easier to find senior saints who have naturally matured in years but not supernaturally into godly fathers. Instead of having forty years of consistent Christian growth, they've had one year of living partially for the Lord, forty times. One of my burdens for writing this book is to motivate a generation of Christians to become spiritual warriors for God according to the standard of His Word.

What will it take to see the church in America please God fully? I believe the answer to this vital question is a commitment on the part of saints to die to self, to have a hunger and thirst to know the Lord intimately, and to mature steadily with each year of life. Daniel changed the world in which he lived through his resolve to please God and not man. Prayerfully reflect upon Daniel 1:8 and the outcome of his life, which mightily influenced kings and nations for God. "But Daniel purposed in his heart that he would not defile himself with the portion of the king's delicacies, nor with the wine which he drank." I dare you to be a Daniel, who purposed in his youth to honor God above man, and to become a biblical father according to John's inspired standards.

CHAPTER SEVEN
SATAN'S METHODS REVEALED

1 JOHN 2:15–17

⸺⸌⸜⸍⸝⸺

A short time after entering the ministry I was asked to visit the home of a married couple that believed that they had a demon-possessed daughter. Whenever I get a call like this, my initial thought is to send the associate pastor to handle the situation. Sadly for me, my current associate pastor, who happens to be my son Kenny, is just now twenty-five years old—so he wasn't quite equipped at age four to handle this matter! To make things worse, I didn't even have an associate pastor then.

I recall the night vividly because I wasn't feeling well—even before I got the call—and it was damp and rainy. (No, I'm not making this up for effect.) In the last chapter I mentioned that most young people and adults have at least one pair of Nike sneakers. Well, I wish I had worn mine on this visit because the young lady who reportedly was controlled by the devil attempted to spit on me repeatedly. This ten-year-old child equipped with anti-pastor saliva missiles had clearly fixed me in her sights. As I dodged the chemical warfare, I thought: Thanks, Lord, for quick feet.

Once the parents placed the child into a temporary holding compartment in her bedroom, I began to probe them about her situation. What I learned from my questions was that both sets of her grandparents were active in the occult, which I believed subjected her to the host of hell. Furthermore, the girl's father didn't know the Lord. Not only that, but she was unclean in both speech and thought, possessing knowledge about sexual matters far beyond the capacity of a normal ten-year old.

This would be my only encounter with the family, since I would subsequently learn that they already had a minister who encouraged them not to see me again. However, God graciously allowed me to lead the father to Christ that night and also permitted these parents to know that they couldn't

65

any longer expose their daughter to their parents' occult practices. I moreover encouraged them to attempt to lead the little one to Christ (as I had also tried on that evening).

One thing became very clear to me on that memorable occasion: Satan is alive and well and seeks to decimate the family. Although he has vast influence over the unsaved, his lurid passion also consists of wrecking the lives of all believers. My brother or sister, get ready to learn about Satan's methods, as revealed in 1 John 2:15–17, and learn how to keep him from gaining a foothold in your life and home:

> Do not love the world or the things in the world. If anyone loves the world, the love of the Father is not in him. For all that *is* in the world—the lust of the flesh, the lust of the eyes, and the pride of life—is not of the Father but is of the world. And the world is passing away, and the lust of it; but he who does the will of God abides forever (1 John 2:15–17).

> Do not love the world nor the things in the world. If anyone loves the world, the love of the Father is not in him. For all that is in the world, the lust of the flesh and the lust of the eyes and the boastful pride of life, is not from the Father, but is from the world. The world is passing away, and *also* its lusts; but the one who does the will of God lives forever (1 John 2:15–17, NASB).

SATAN'S APPEAL TO HIS THREE AMIGOS—F

- What is the "world," as mentioned several times in 1 John 2:15–17?
- What biblical principle can be derived from 1 John 2:15?
- Why specifically does John give the three enticements of the world as "the lust of the flesh and the lust of the eyes and the pride of life" in 1 John 2:16?
- How does John contrast the temporal versus the eternal in 1 John 2:17?

SATAN'S APPEAL TO HIS THREE AMIGOS—I

The church at Ephesus had moved in the wrong spiritual direction, so John wrote, "Do not love the world or the things in the world" (1 John 2:15). The apostle of love used the present imperative, most likely signifying that the Ephesians needed to halt and no longer love this world's system. The "world," as used throughout this passage, means Satan's rule over this world's order, which opposes God's ways, and promotes "the lust of the flesh, the lust of the eyes, and the pride of life" (1 John 2:16).

John clearly showed that one couldn't latch onto this world's *modus operandi* and God at the same time. He logically concluded, "If anyone loves the world, the love of the Father is not in him" (1 John 2:15b). This world's system and God are mutually exclusive.

Next John gave the reason why believers have nothing in common with anything headed by Satan. "For all that *is* in the world—the lust of the flesh, the lust of the eyes, and the pride of life—is not of the Father but is of the world" (1 John 2:16). The Greek word for "lust" is neutral; the context determines if it is a good or bad desire. "The lust of the flesh" refers to that indwelling principle of sin that the believer inherited from Adam. The devil appeals to man's fallen nature, since this is one of his three key allies (or amigos, as I am calling them).

The wicked one's next comrade consists of "the lust of the eyes." John understood that Satan loves to entice people with visual aids; he wants to have believing eyes come in contact with those things that will cause him or her to stumble. Finally, his third partner in crime is "the pride of life." Satan desires the child of God not to depend upon the Lord for divine enablement but rather to pull himself up by his own bootstraps and then personally take all the credit for his accomplishments. Since the devil fell because of pride, he longs for the saints to arrogantly pursue life without God's help.

What the prince of darkness doesn't want disclosed throughout his allurements arises in 1 John 2:17, "And the world is passing away, and the lust of it; but he who does the will of God abides forever." John captures why God's children should weigh their options by showing that this world's system currently "is passing away." We shouldn't run after the temporal, but rather, pursue the eternal.

In particular, what lasts forever and should be sought after passionately? John wrote, "He who does the will of God abides forever." "Does" is a present tense participle, showing a continual conviction to practice the will of God. The apostle articulated that the believer models that he's born again because he carries out the Father's bidding and "abides forever." "Abides" is another present tense verb showing the staying or lasting power of God's child—for all of eternity.

This portion of Scripture has broad implications. We will see how Satan used these tactics on Adam and Eve, and subsequently upon Jesus, as we review relationship.

SATAN'S APPEAL TO HIS THREE AMIGOS—R

My dear friend, Jesus said in Matthew 6:24, "No one can serve two masters; for either he will hate the one and love the other, or else he will be loyal to the one and despise the other. You cannot serve God and mammon [material possessions]." This timeless truth applies to 1 John 2:15; you cannot love God and this world's system simultaneously. Like oil and water, they don't mix. John plainly stated, "If anyone loves the world, the love of the Father is not in Him."

Knowing that John specifically described this world's system as pertaining to "the lust of the flesh, the lust of the eyes, and the pride of life," why did he mention just these three components? The answer seems to be because these are the three attractions that the world continually features, and Satan has used them consistently to decoy God's people away from Him since the beginning of time.

Let's consider how the wicked one approached Eve in the Garden of Eden in Genesis 3. First, Satan questioned the authority of God's Word. Hear the deceiver ply his trade by the subtle question he asked, after God had told Adam and Eve not to partake of the tree of the knowledge of good and evil: "Has God indeed said, 'You shall not eat of every tree of the garden'?" (Gen. 3:1). From there, he denies the truth of God's Word and then implies that He's not good. "And the serpent said to the woman, 'You will not surely die. For God knows that in the day you eat of it [the fruit from the tree of the knowledge of good and evil] your eyes will be opened, and you will be like God, knowing good and evil'" (Gen. 3:4–5).

Eve, lamentably, was duped by Satan's trickery, while Adam sinned with eyes wide open. Can you pick out the lust of the flesh and the lust of the eyes and the pride of life from Genesis 3:6–7? "So when the woman saw that the tree was good for food, that it was pleasant to the eyes, and a tree desirable to make *one* wise, she took of its fruit and ate. She also gave to her husband with her, and he ate. Then the eyes of both of them were opened, and they knew that they *were* naked; and they sewed fig leaves together and made themselves coverings."

Let's see how you did. The "food" of verse 6 connected with "the lust of the flesh," and being "pleasant to the eyes" related to "the lust of the eyes." Finally, "to make *one* wise" became the appeal to "the pride of life" (verse 6). Satan might change the packaging on his three universal pieces of bait; however, he uses the same general tactics regularly. As a consequence of Adam's disobedience, sin entered into the world, with its end result of death.

Spring forward thousands of years, and observe the devil trying to seduce the Lord Jesus with his proven techniques. We could study either Matthew 4 or Luke 4, since both gospels cover this account. Matthew's gospel seems to contain the temptations in the order that they occurred, as it uses the Greek word for "at that time" four times (verses 1, 5, 10, and 11), while Luke apparently topically arranged his version. We'll follow Dr. Luke's research, since he gave the story in the same order of John's warning about the lust of the flesh and the lust of the eyes and the pride of life.

As Luke begins his record, he reveals the importance of the Spirit in the believer's life to experience victory over Satan's temptations: "Then Jesus, being filled with the Holy Spirit, returned from the Jordan and was led by the Spirit into the wilderness" (Luke 4:1). After Jesus' forty-day fast, the deceiver began his maneuvers. The ruler of darkness understood whom he was seeking to beguile. The conditional assertion "if" consists of a first-class condition assuming the statement to be true. "If [since] You are the Son of God, command this stone to become bread" (Luke 4:3). Although Jesus didn't have a sin nature for Satan to appeal to, our Lord could be tempted (see Hebrews 4:15). Knowing this, the devil plied his deceptions, so that Jesus might submit to "the lust of the flesh."

After Jesus quotes Deuteronomy 8:3, showing that man needs not just bread for survival but all of God's Word, Satan took "Him up on a high mountain, [and] showed Him all the kingdoms of the world in a moment of time" (Luke 4:5). This supernatural display was to entice Jesus to succumb to "the lust of the eyes." Thankfully our Lord, who created the heavens and the earth, knew that this world's system was on borrowed time and shouldn't be adored. Jesus quotes Deuteronomy for the second time, demanding, "Get behind Me, Satan! For it is written, 'You shall worship the LORD your God, and Him only you shall serve'" (Luke 4:8).

The devil immediately had one more trick up his sleeve. He took Jesus up to the southeast corner of the temple known as the pinnacle (meaning "little wing") overlooking the Kidron Valley. In essence, Satan wanted Jesus to jump and allow His angels to rescue Him so that He could then boast about His authority over the angelic realm. (This temptation points to "the pride of life.") Satan conveniently quotes most of Psalm 91:11–12 to Jesus: "For it is written: 'He shall give His angels charge over You, to keep You,' and, in their hands they shall bear You up, Lest you dash your foot against a stone.'" He left out the words "in all your ways" after "to keep you" in Psalm 91:11, and twisted the meaning of the passage from trusting God to tempting Him. Jesus then once more quotes Deuteronomy (6:16), "It has been said, 'You shall not tempt the LORD your God'" (Luke 4:12). If Jesus had fallen for any of Satan's offers, we could not have been saved; Jesus would no longer have been the spotless Lamb of God. Thank God that Jesus followed the Father in all His ways.

Now that we've looked at Satan's devices, let's see how 1 John 2:15–17 should be applied, so that we don't give in to the triad of seductive temporal pleasures.

SATAN'S APPEAL TO HIS THREE AMIGOS—E

Our first employment point comes from 1 John 2:15: *Stop loving the world and serve only Jesus.* Honesty would require all of us to acknowledge that, more often than we'd like to admit, we've been seduced by the lust of the flesh and the lust of the eyes and the pride of life. The authoritative Word of God, however, commands us to offer our full allegiance to Jesus.

The Jewish historian Flavius Josephus reported that eighty-three high priests served from the days of Aaron, the first high priest, until the destruction of the temple in AD 70. But unlike the other high priests who first offered a sacrifice for their own sins on the Day of Atonement and then for the people, Jesus offered Himself. This High Priest not only laid His life down for us but also took it up again.

Consider *His Preeminent Priesthood* as recorded in Hebrews 4:14, "Seeing then that we have [a present tense verb, showing that Jesus continues to serve in this capacity] a great High Priest who has passed through the heavens, Jesus the Son of God, let us hold fast *our* confession" (Heb. 4:14). Knowing that we have Jesus representing and praying for us before the Father should, in and of itself, motivate us to stop loving the world.

Not only should we marvel at *His Preeminent Priesthood* but moreover at *His Perfect Person.* Hebrews 4:15 shares, "For we do not have a High Priest who cannot sympathize with our weaknesses, but was in all points tempted as *we are*, yet without sin." Turn to the *Perfect Person* when Satan hurls his temptations at you.

Furthermore, we need to marvel at *His Punctual Provision*, which always arrives on time. "Let us therefore come boldly to the throne of grace, that we may obtain mercy and find grace to help in time of need" (Heb. 4:16). So, my treasured brother or sister in Christ, *Stop loving the world and serve only Jesus.*

The second application, from 1 John 2:16, gives us necessary information to understand where our enchantments come from: *The allurements of the world aren't from God.* John tells us, "the lust of the flesh, the lust of the eyes, and the pride of life—is not of the Father but is of the world."

Enticements don't originate from God; He might choose to test us, but He'll never tempt us. The half-brother of our Lord emphatically stated, "Let no one say when he is tempted, 'I am tempted by God,' for God cannot be tempted by evil, nor does He Himself tempt anyone" (James 1:13). Jesus, who became like us so ultimately we could become like Him, could be tempted as the God-Man. That is why we turn to Him as our victorious champion when this world comes calling.

Child of God, understand that Satan has an ally in each of us because of our sin nature inherited from Adam. That's why James continued, "But each one is tempted when he is drawn away by his own desires and enticed. Then, when desire has conceived, it gives birth to sin; and sin, when it is full-grown, brings forth death. Do not be deceived my beloved brethren" (James 1:14–16). Don't flirt with temptation; when it is embraced, it leads you down the pathway to death. Wisely use the knowledge that 1 John 2:16 gives you.

Our third employment point, from 1 John 2:17, is: *Don't toy with the temporal, but toil with the Eternal One.* John contrasted that which is passing away with the individual who won't, "And the world is passing away, and the lust of it; but he who does the will of God abides forever."

Moses, the Man of God, understood the difference between that which is passing away and the eternal. The writer of Hebrews said about Moses who communed with God face to face, "choosing rather to suffer affliction with the people of God than to enjoy the passing pleasures of sin, esteeming the reproach of Christ greater riches than the treasures in Egypt; for he looked to the reward" (Heb. 11:25–27). I pray, dear child of God, that you will grasp the eternal like Moses did.

Jesus made a fascinating connection in the passage dealing with His temptations: He said, "Get behind Me, Satan! For it is written, 'You shall worship the LORD your God, and Him only you shall serve'" (Luke 4:8). Whomever you choose to worship, that will be the one you serve. My appeal to you is this: *Don't toy with the temporal but toil with the Eternal One.*

CHAPTER EIGHT

DETECTING THE SPIRIT OF ANTICHRIST

1 JOHN 2:18–27

⋙∿〰⋘

Walking up to the front door of a big farmhouse, a hobo knocked lightly on the door until the owner answered. The hobo said, "Please, sir, could I have something to eat? I haven't had a meal in days." The well-dressed homeowner said, "I have made a fortune supplying goods to people, but I never give away anything for nothing. However, if you go around the back of the house, you'll find a gallon of paint and a clean brush. Paint my porch and I'll give you a good meal."

The hobo headed off to the back of the house, and a few hours later he came back to knock on the door again. The homeowner was surprised. "Finished already? That's great! Come on in and sit down, and I'll have the cook bring you a meal!"

"Thank you, sir!" the hobo said. "I should tell you though, that you don't know your cars. That's not a Porsche. It's a BMW."

Mistakes can be costly. Yet, to paint a "Porsche" instead of a "porch" only affects the material. To mistakenly follow an antichrist has eternal consequences. John had just written in 1 John 2:17 that the "world is passing away." Let's see how we can know this, from 1 John 2:18–27:

> Little children, it is the last hour; and as you have heard that the Antichrist is coming, even now many antichrists have come, by which we know that it is the last hour. They went out from us, but they were not of us; for if they had been of us, they would have continued with us; but *they went out* that they might be made manifest, that none of them were of us.

But you have an anointing from the Holy One, and you know all things. I have not written to you because you do not know the truth, but because you know it, and that no lie is of the truth.

Who is a liar but he who denies that Jesus is the Christ? He is antichrist who denies the Father and the Son. Whoever denies the Son does not have the Father either; he who acknowledges the Son has the Father also.

Therefore let that abide in you which you heard from the beginning. If what you heard from the beginning abides in you, you also will abide in the Son and in the Father. And this is the promise that He has promised us—eternal life.

These things I have written to you concerning those who *try to* deceive you. But the anointing which you have received from Him abides in you, and you do not need that anyone teach you; but as the same anointing teaches you concerning all things, and is true, and is not a lie, and just as it has taught you, you will abide in Him (1 John 2:18–27).

Children, it is the last hour, and just as you heard that the antichrist is coming, so now many antichrists have appeared. We know from this that it is the last hour. They went out from us, but they did not really belong to us, because if they had belonged to us, they would have remained with us. But they went out from us to demonstrate that all of them do not belong to us.

Nevertheless you have an anointing from the Holy One, and you all know. I have not written to you that you do not know the truth, but that you do know it, and that no lie is of the truth. Who is the liar but the person who denies that Jesus is the Christ? This one is the antichrist: the person who denies the Father and the Son. Everyone who denies the Son does not have the Father either. The person who confesses the Son has the Father also.

As for you, what you have heard from the beginning must remain in you. If what you heard from the beginning remains in you, you also will remain in the Son and in the Father. Now this is the promise that he himself made to us: eternal life. These things I have written to you about those who are trying to deceive you.

Now as for you, the anointing that you received from him resides in you, and you have no need for anyone to teach you. But as his anointing teaches you about all things, it is true and is not a lie. Just as it has taught you, you reside in him (1 John 2:18–27, NET).

TAKING ON THE BIBLICAL ROLE OF SHERLOCK HOLMES—F

- What is "the last hour" referring to in 1 John 2:18?
- What's the difference between "the Antichrist" and "many antichrists" in 1 John 2:18?
- What is the "anointing from the Holy One" in 1 John 2:20?
- What were believers to let "abide in you which you heard from the beginning" in 1 John 2:24?
- First John 2:27 says "and you don't need that anyone teach you." Does this mean that Bible teachers aren't necessary?

TAKING ON THE BIBLICAL ROLE OF SHERLOCK HOLMES—I

As in 1 John 2:12, John addresses this paragraph to the "little children." He informed his flock "it is the last hour; and as you have heard that the Antichrist is coming." The expression "it is the last hour" clearly doesn't refer to a literal hour, since we are 2,000 years removed from John's day and the Antichrist who "is coming" didn't emerge in the first century. "The last hour" points to the period of time between Jesus' first and second comings.

John apparently had given instruction about the Man of Sin to his congregation since he wrote, "and as you have heard that the Antichrist is coming" (1 John 2:18). The prefix "anti" can mean "in place of" or "against." The future emissary of Satan will oppose both the person and work of Jesus, the Christ.

John added, "even now many antichrists have come by which we know that it is the last hour." John knew experientially (the inference of the Greek verb "know" in verse 18) that the forerunners of the future Antichrist were already on the scene, and no doubt, God's choice servant had confronted many about their heretical teachings. Good shepherds actively watch over their flocks, and purge the wolves when they are detected. They need to, because Satan learned ages ago concerning the church: If you can't beat her, join her. I'm sure that the former "son of thunder" was instrumental in driving out the wolves.

John then wisely shared why the wolves had to go: "They went out from us, but they were not of us; for if they had been of us, they would have continued with us" (1 John 2:19). John had spent time with Judas and understood firsthand how a Christian imposter lived. John then adds a condition of the second class—using "if" with the concept of assuming something not to be true—when he penned, "for if they had been of us, they would have continued with us." By this, he shows that those who left the church didn't know Jesus.

John continues, "but they went out that they might be made manifest that none of them were of us" (1 John 2:19). Their departure demonstrated that it wasn't just a change of church they sought, but rather that they had abandoned the faith. The mark of the genuine believer consists of enduring in the Christian faith until the end. Not one of those who jumped ship was saved, and their apostasy showcased an unbelieving shipwrecked life.

In contrast to those who left the true church of Jesus Christ, John offered, "But you [believers] have an anointing from the Holy One, and you know all things" (1 John 2:20). How were the believers anointed? They received God's Holy Spirit at their conversion. The Spirit of God enabled them to discern truth from error, and that's why John wrote, "and you know all things." The following verses elaborate upon this inner knowledge.

The "all things" pertain to doctrinal matters concerning the person of Jesus. First John 2:21 declares, "I have not written to you because you do not know the truth, but because you know it, and that no lie is of the truth." The individuals who exited the church held to Gnostic tendencies, which misrepresented Jesus' nature. John confirmed that the believers who stayed had the discernment not to be duped by falsehoods.

Indeed, John asks and answers in 1 John 2:22, "Who is a liar but he who denies that Jesus is the Christ? He is antichrist who denies the Father and the Son." The denial "that Jesus is the Christ" is probably a reference to Cerinthian Gnosticism, which held that after Jesus' baptism He was infused with divine power that came upon Him, but which departed from Him prior to the crucifixion. The liar is pegged as an "antichrist who denies the Father and the Son." "Denies" occurs in the present tense and shows a habitual denial.

John then switched the order from Father and Son, to Son and Father, in verse 23: "Whoever denies the Son does not have the Father either; he who acknowledges the Son has the Father also." No one can arrive in heaven and bypass the Son; but to know the Son personally is to have a relationship with the Father also.

Transitioning forward, John then gave a command, "Therefore let that abide in you which you heard from the beginning" (1 John 2:24). What had the receivers of John's epistle "heard from the beginning" that was to remain with them? They had heard the gospel, and now must continue to dwell upon God's Word so not to be led astray. The good news is exactly that according to 1 John 2:25, "And this is the promise that He has promised us—eternal life." "Eternal life" had already begun in the believer from the moment he or she embraced that life-changing message and would culminate with the reality of being in Jesus' physical presence.

The implications are enormous concerning the gospel; therefore, John warns his sheep, "These things I have written concerning those who try to deceive you" (1 John 2:26). John exposed that not only had these antichrists left the church, but that they were attempting to lead Christians astray. These purveyors of deception desired believers to wander from doctrinal stability to the realm of spiritual disaster.

John closes out this section with, "But the anointing which you have received from Him abides in you, and you don't need that anyone teach you" 1 John 2:27). He primarily refers to the false teachers, whom they didn't need for training, and subsequently states, "but as the same anointing teaches you concerning all things, and is true, and is not a lie, and just as it has taught you, you will abide in Him." The indwelling Holy Spirit should be the guide to understanding God's Word (because He directs us to reside in Jesus), and not those who inaccurately represent Him.

TAKING ON THE BIBLICAL ROLE OF SHERLOCK HOLMES—R

When John mentions, "it is the last hour," he uses an eschatological term, which comprises the period between the first and second comings of Jesus. It is equivalent to Paul's "last days" in 2 Timothy 3:1. This "last hour" or "last days" began with Jesus' first coming. Read carefully Hebrews 1:1-2a: "God, who at various times and in different ways spoke in time past to the fathers by the prophets, has in these last days spoken to us by *His* Son." The last days began at Jesus' first advent, and will end prior to the time known as the tribulation as described in Revelation 6–19, when Jesus returns for the church at the rapture.

What does the Bible teach about the Antichrist? He's called the "man of sin" and "the son of perdition" in 2 Thessalonians 2:3. After Jesus returns for the church, this man, energized by Satan, will make a covenant with the nation of Israel for seven years (see Daniel 9:24–27). In the middle of their contractual agreement, he will breach the covenant, and proclaim that he's truly God in the future temple, which will be built in Jerusalem.

Paul described his activities further in 2 Thessalonians 2:4, "who opposes and exalts himself above all that is called God or that is worshipped, so that he sits as God in the temple of God, showing himself that he is God." The apostle John captured his movements in the second half of the tribulation, known as the great tribulation, in Revelation 13:5–6: "And he was given a mouth speaking great things and blasphemies, and he was given authority to continue for forty-two months. Then he opened his mouth in blasphemy against God, to blaspheme His name, His tabernacle, and those who dwell in heaven."

Currently the spirit of antichrist emanates through those whose message rejects the deity of Jesus, and is propagated by those dubbed by John as antichrists. Today these antichrists can be viewed as those who are setting the stage for the Antichrist.

John subsequently contrasted those false messengers commissioned by

Satan—the Antichrist and antichrists—with the true: "But you have an anointing from the Holy One, and you know all things" (1 John 2:20). We saw that the anointing came from God's Holy Spirit, who indwells all believers. The Holy Spirit is associated with anointing throughout the Scriptures. There are biblical examples of prophets, priests, and kings being anointed with oil. For instance, 1 Samuel 16:13 reports, "Then Samuel took the horn of oil and anointed him [David] in the midst of his brothers; and the Spirit of the LORD came upon David." Our Lord also received an anointing: "how God anointed Jesus of Nazareth with the Holy Spirit and power" (Acts 10:38).

Since we have been anointed and "know all things" (1 John 2:20), and "do not need that anyone teach you" (1 John 2:27), does John contradict Paul, who wrote about Jesus, "And He Himself gave some *to be* apostles, some prophets, some evangelists, and some pastors and teachers for the equipping of the saints for the work of ministry" (Eph. 4:11–12a)? The short answer is no. An imperative to Bible study is knowing the context of any passage. A review of both contexts shows that the two apostles' teachings were not at odds.

First John 2:20 expresses that "you know all things" because God's Spirit resides within every believer. Since He's "the Spirit of truth," according to John 16:13, He also "will guide you into all truth." In essence, the Holy Spirit exits within each believer as a lie detector, and helps us to know the true from the false as stated in 1 John 2:21: "I have not written to you because you do not know the truth, but because you know it, and that no lie is of the truth." Both occurrences of "know" in 1 John 2:21 relate to intuitive knowledge, meaning their internal comprehension derived via the Holy Spirit.

Paul, on the other hand, showed that Jesus gave gifted men to the church in order to give instruction to the saints for the maturation of the body of Christ. Our Lord still today uses godly teachers to give necessary information to believers who have an inner confirmation of that truth by the Holy Spirit. The two passages most definitely don't contradict but complement one another.

Now that we've become familiar with 1 John 2:18–27, have also interpreted the passage, and related it to relevant passages, it is now time to employ it. I trust that you are ready to go to work.

TAKING ON THE BIBLICAL ROLE OF SHERLOCK HOLMES—E

We have been in the last days for 2,000 years. One thing hasn't changed over two millennia: *Antichrists will abandon the church during the last days.* That becomes our first employment point, derived from 1 John 2:18–19. Our first point is informational in nature and helps us to understand what is happening in churches all around the world. These individuals would probably have stayed in the church if it weren't for doctrinally solid men like John who confronted them.

Remember that Satan knows that he can't defeat the church—so he's joined the ranks. Jude forewarned us with this insight, "Beloved, while I was very diligent to write to you concerning our common salvation, I found it necessary to write to you exhorting you to contend earnestly for the faith which was once for all delivered to the saints. For certain men have crept in unnoticed, who long ago were marked out for this condemnation, ungodly men, who turn the grace of our God into licentiousness and deny the only Lord God and our Lord Jesus Christ" (Jude 3–4).

Dear child of God, please don't assume that everyone who attends church with you believes in Jesus. The devil's nature has a bent toward destruction, and he loves to wreak havoc on the lives of the saints through those he has planted within the church. For this reason, *let God's Spirit discern truth and lies*—our second employment point, rooted in 1 John 2:20–23. This is why John wrote, "I have not written to you because you do not know the truth, but because you know it, and that no lie is of the truth" (1 John 2:21). God also has planted someone within the church, and within every believer; the Holy Spirit resides within you to help you detect truth from lies.

The key question to proffer when trying to decide if someone is a genuine believer is: Who is Jesus Christ? John pointedly got to the bottom of this issue when he wrote, "Who is a liar but he who denies that Jesus is the Christ? He is antichrist who denies the Father and the Son" (1 John 2:22).

He further builds his case, "Whoever denies the Son does not have the Father either; he who acknowledges the Son has the Father also" (1 John 2:23). Later John would add in 1 John 4:1, "Beloved, do not believe every spirit, but test the spirits, whether they are of God; because many false prophets have gone out into the world." Don't forget: *Let God's Spirit discern truth and lies.*

How can you remain in the realm of God's Spirit so that you have good discernment? *Let God's Spirit and Word instruct you continually* is our third employment point, derived from 1 John 2:24–27. Having a daily Bible reading, meditating upon that text, and sitting under solid biblical teaching will give you the necessary tools to spot a spiritual "phony baloney."

Paul commanded the Colossian saints, "Let the word of Christ dwell in you richly" (Col. 3:16). Concerning the gospel, and by way of applying God's Word in its entirety, John builds upon this sage advice in 1 John 2:24, "Therefore let that abide in you which you heard from the beginning. If what you heard from the beginning abides in you, you also will abide in the Son and in the Father." The Bible planted deeply in the heart of the believer, when applied, will keep every child of God walking with God. Hence the Holy Spirit, who illuminates our minds to comprehend the Scripture, will keep us abiding in truth because we're fellowshipping with both the Father and the Son.

Let's review our three application points. *Antichrists will abandon the church during the last days.* Therefore, *let God's Spirit discern truth and lies.* And finally, *let God's Spirit and Word instruct you continually.* Be aware and discerning, my fellow soldier in Christ.

PART TWO
REACTIONS FROM FELLOWSHIP

1 JOHN 2:28–5:21

CHAPTER NINE

THE IMPLICATIONS OF JESUS' IMMINENT RETURN

1 JOHN 2:28–3:3

―――∽∧∿――

Have you ever had to appear before a judge? I did, and may I say that it doesn't rank high on my list of fond memories. Maybe like you, I believed on Jesus but didn't have a spiritual mentor to guide my path in righteousness. Today I share with my congregation—when I want to remind them that I didn't always walk with Jesus as a Christian should—that I haven't had a drink since I've become the legal age, and that I also haven't caused a car accident since I got my license. Now that I've shared those details: The reason I had to stand before a judge was because I caused a car accident and didn't have a driver's license.

Although I didn't have a valid license, I'd done a fair amount of driving prior to my wreck. I took turns driving to both North Carolina and Florida from Maryland with a friend and never had an incident. However, the Lord wanted to get my attention.

It was a rainy night; my buddy and I were about thirty minutes from home in his vehicle because he had a brief appointment. As we approached our destination, he noticed that there weren't any parking spaces on either side of the street; therefore, he asked me to sit in the driver's seat and drive around the block if another vehicle approached. After he exited the vehicle, a car approached from the rear. I put the Plymouth in drive and planned to go around the block; however, I ran a stop sign and had a large Lincoln Continental smash into the driver's side door. (I can still see the horrified woman's face today.) Thankfully no one was hurt, but you can imagine my friend's response when he saw his beautiful car with a new design and a police officer now talking to me.

That night my friend and I headed home to break the news to my folks. Did I mention that my father was a District of Columbia police officer, and that I now had to give an account to Lieutenant Burge? Once my quivering voice shared the news, he promptly turned to my mom and said, "Your son just wrecked his best friend's car."

Needless to say, the Lord got my attention. I remember telling Him that I was now going to faithfully live for Him, and that there would be no turning back. I can truly report that when I went to court that I had a peace. Jesus' words from Luke 9:62 became real to me from the second of my accident, "No one, having put his hand to the plow, and looking back, is fit for the kingdom of God." Not only had God miraculously protected me in what could (and probably should) have been a fatal car crash, but also in court. First, the lady who plowed into my buddy's car didn't show up to testify. Moreover, the policeman who wrote the accident report was also missing in action. As a result, the judge gave me a friendly but much-deserved lecture, and I received probation.

My friend, there will come a day when we all will appear before Jesus, our Judge. Are you ready to stand before the One who knows not only everything we've ever done, but the motives behind our actions? Let's prayerfully read 1 John 2:28–3:3, which when applied will prepare us to stand before Christ's judgment seat:

> And now, little children, abide in Him, that when He appears, we may have confidence and not be ashamed before Him at His coming. If you know that He is righteous, you know that everyone who practices righteousness is born of Him.
>
> Behold what manner of love the Father has bestowed on us, that we should be called children of God! Therefore the world does not know us, because it did not know Him. Beloved, now we are children of God; and it has not yet been revealed what we shall be, but we know that when He is revealed, we shall be like Him, for we shall see Him as He is. And everyone who has this hope in Him purifies himself, just as He is pure (1 John 2:28–3:3).

Children, stay one in your hearts with Christ. Then when he returns, we will have confidence and won't have to hide in shame. You know that Christ always does right and that everyone who does right is a child of God.

Think how much the Father loves us. He loves us so much that he lets us be called his children, as we truly are. But since the people of this world did not know who Christ is, they don't know who we are. My dear friends, we are already God's children, though what we will be hasn't yet been seen. But we do know that when Christ returns, we will be like him, because we will see him as he truly is. This hope makes us keep ourselves holy, just as Christ is holy (1 John 2:28–3:3, CEV).

PREPARE TO MEET YOUR MAKER—F

- Why did John include himself when he wrote "we may have confidence," when speaking about Jesus' return in 1 John 2:28?
- What does the word "confidence" literally mean?
- How will some believers be "ashamed" when Jesus returns, as stated in 1 John 2:28?
- When "shall we see Him [Jesus] as He is" from 1 John 3:2?
- What is the believer's hope, based upon from 1 John 3:3?

PREPARE TO MEET YOUR MAKER—I

In the first part of this epistle, John gave us many *reasons for fellowship* rooted in Jesus' personhood, which pertained to doctrinal matters. Now that we know what to believe, we need to act upon the earlier information shared in this profound book, from which further *reactions from fellowship* occur. Like other New Testament epistles, first the doctrine is laid out and then the application.

John marks the beginning of our new section with the words "and now." He then commanded his dear little children to "abide in Him." The present tense imperative ("abide") requires that these saints continually reside, or continue to walk, with Jesus. This way, "when He appears, we may have confidence and not be ashamed before Him at His coming" (1 John 2:28). The question isn't "if" Jesus will return—He certainly will—but "when" He'll return.

John gives a purpose for preparing for Jesus' coming, "that when He appears, we may have confidence and not be ashamed before Him at His coming." "Confidence" derives from a compound Greek word meaning "all speech." The idea conveys that the believer will have a freedom of speech upon meeting Jesus, because he or she has been remaining in Him. The believer who abides in Jesus can have the ability to converse boldly with Jesus when He returns. On the other hand, the child of God who doesn't walk with Jesus will be put to shame when He makes His appearance.

Next, the apostle wrote in 1 John 2:29, "If you know that He is righteous, you know that everyone who practices righteousness is born of Him." Scholars debate whether "He" refers to God or Jesus. Jesus was clearly described in the previous verse, but the end of the same verse decidedly points to the Father who regenerates the lost and makes them born again. Either way, both the Father and the Son are righteous, and the individual who does righteousness testifies by his deeds that he is a child of God.

As we transition to a new chapter, I'd like to remind you that when the Bible was originally written that it didn't have chapter and verse divisions. Therefore, I believe that 1 John 3:1–3 are a part of a larger unit that began in 1 John 2:28. Hence, John continues with "Behold what manner of love the Father has bestowed on us, that we should be called children of God!" (1 John 3:1). The imperative "Behold" means to stop and look. The saints were to contemplate this most unusual love. God's love, in essence, is out of this world, not just from a distant land. John would have us puzzle "that we should be called children of God." Since we belong to God, "Therefore the world does not know us, because it did not know Him."

John then picks up the result of Jesus' return for His own: "Beloved, now we are children of God; and it has not yet been revealed what we shall be, but we know that when He is revealed, we shall be like Him, for we shall see Him as He is" (1 John 3:2). Those whom God the Father loved (3:1) are also loved by John; he called them "beloved." The word "now" sets up a contrast between the believer's current status as a "child of God" and our future resemblance to Jesus.

There are no snapshots of what our future glorified bodies will look like. That's why John wrote, "it has not yet been revealed what we shall be." However, the best is yet to come because "when [not "if"] He is revealed, we shall be like Him, for we shall see Him as He is." We'll look further into our instantaneous transformation when we get into relationship.

There exists an immediate application to our future change: "And everyone who has this hope in Him, purifies himself, just as He is pure" (1 John 3:3). Everyone who lives in light of the imminent return of Christ experiences a purification process. The "hope" speaks of the rapture, and the words, "in him" literally are "on Him" or "upon Him." Therefore, the believer who carries upon himself the expectation of Christ's immediate return "purifies himself." The Greek verb for "purifies" emerges in the present tense; we keep on purifying ourselves "just as He [Christ] is pure."

There exists so much wonderful information in these five verses. Let's unpack their fuller meaning.

PREPARE TO MEET YOUR MAKER—R

Since we know that Jesus will return, when will He come? First, let me make a distinction between the rapture and the second coming of Jesus Christ. The rapture can occur at any moment, whereas the second coming of Jesus Christ is a subsequent event and doesn't take place until the tribulation period (described in Revelation 6–19) is over. We will meet the Lord in the air when He returns for the church at the rapture, according to 1 Thessalonians 4:17; but Jesus will physically descend upon the earth, at the Mount of Olives, when He returns the second time, according to Zechariah 14:4.

Today, there's much chatter about the signs that need to happen before Jesus comes. This statement is true when pertaining to the second coming but not the rapture. Many signs occur in Revelation 6–19 and other places in the Bible such as Matthew 24 that describe certain events pointing to Jesus' second coming. Yet there are no signs that need to transpire before the rapture.

Both Paul and John believed that they could be alive when Jesus returned, approximately 2,000 years ago. Paul states in 1 Thessalonians 4:15, "For this we say to you by the word of the Lord, that we who are alive and remain until the coming of the Lord will by no means precede those who are asleep." Paul's use of "we" testified that he could be among those raptured, which would not occur before the dead in Christ were raised. Again in 1 Thessalonians 4:17, "Then we who are alive and remain shall be caught up together with them [those who died during the church age, whose souls and spirits are already with Jesus according to 2 Corinthians 5:8] in the clouds to meet the Lord in the air. And thus we shall always be with the Lord."

John gives the same witness about the imminent return of Jesus. Observe the "we" in 1 John 2:28: "And now, little children, abide in Him, that when He appears, we may have confidence and not be ashamed before Him at His coming." Both Paul and John had assurance that they could be among those who would be raptured. If the rapture didn't occur in the first century, how much closer must we be to this blessed event?

With this confidence, John declares, "And everyone who has this hope in Him, purifies himself, just as He is pure" (1 John 3:3). Believer, our hope, based upon the historical facts of Jesus' death and resurrection, should greatly affect us daily. Paul wrote, "*There is* one body [the church] and one Spirit, just as you were called in one hope of your calling" (Eph. 4:4). The rapture should become each Christian's personal hope.

This hope doesn't include any uncertainly about the rapture. Jesus' return is as certain as the historicity of Jesus' death and resurrection. Paul uses a first class condition, assuming the "if" to be true, in 1 Thessalonians 4:14: "For if [or since] we believe that Jesus died and rose again, even so God will bring with Him those who sleep in Jesus." The verbs "died" and "rose again" are in the active voice, showing that no one took Jesus' life and caused Him to rise again, which would have been indicated by passive verbs. Rather, He laid down His own life and raised it back up again, as He predicted in John 10:17–18. Since He had the authority to do these things (on our behalf), He will return for us as promised because He's demonstrated that He has the power to fulfill His Word.

Furthermore, the apostle Paul builds upon this concept of hope in Titus 2:13–14, "looking for the blessed hope and glorious appearing of our great God and Savior Jesus Christ, who gave Himself for us, that ["that" speaks of purpose] He might redeem us from every lawless deed and purify for Himself *His* own special people, zealous for good works." Deliberate, regular reflection upon Jesus' imminent return produces a cleansing in the believer's life and provides the motivation to serve Him diligently.

Let's consider the implications, both positive and negative, from the mandate to "abide in Him," so that "we may have confidence and not be ashamed before Him at His coming" (1 John 2:28). Both John and Paul believed that they could be alive at the rapture. When you, my friend, walk closely with Jesus, you can have a freedom of discourse with Him and not shrink back from seeing Him at His appearing. When Jesus returns for us we'll be judged at the bema seat. Second Corinthians 5:10 announces, "For we must all appear before the judgment seat of Christ, that each one may receive the things *done* in the body, according to what he has done, whether good or bad." The judgment or bema seat refers to a raised platform that judges would sit upon to render decisions on court cases. This is how our judgment is depicted, with Jesus being our Judge (see John 5:22).

Paul elaborates upon both our judgment and our reward in 1 Corinthians 3. At the rapture, "each one's work will become manifest, for the Day will declare it, because it will be revealed by fire; and the fire will test each one's work, of what sort it is. If anyone's work which he has built on it endures, he will receive a reward" (1 Cor. 3:13–14). Conversely, if the child of God mixed bad doctrine with impure motives, there would be a cost: "If anyone's work is burned, he will suffer loss; but he himself will be saved, yet so as through fire" (1 Cor. 3:15).

Abiding in Christ requires us to keep our lives pure, so that the works we produce will yield rewards that will remain under Jesus' future scrutiny. Jesus paid for your sins at the cross; you'll never be judged for them. Nonetheless, your life's work will come under the discerning eye of Jesus. You've been saved in order to serve God, according to Ephesians 2:10. As you walk with Jesus, allow Him to keep your life blameless and your motives for service pure, so that you stand approved before Him.

Okay, it's time again to put into action what we've studied. There are no unemployment lines for God's children. Let's roll up our sleeves and get to work.

PREPARE TO MEET YOUR MAKER—E

Walk with Jesus for boldness at His appearance, from 1 John 2:28, is our first employment point. I recall my last assignment working for the telephone company around 1988. It was in that same year that I had been ordained and was serving part-time as the associate pastor in our church. I had requested to begin my job at 7:00 a.m. so that I could be home mid-afternoon to focus upon my ministry. The management didn't start work until around 8:00 a.m., so non-management personnel weren't permitted to start before that time. Yet somehow, I had been granted that permission.

One early morning, I heard someone outside my office. (It was unusual for anyone to be around the office at that time, except me.) It turned out to be an upper-level manager, whose investigation revealed me working promptly and diligently by 7:00 a.m. at my desk. I never had worried about a surprise visit because I worked for the Lord and knew He always watched my activity. I had confidence at my manager's early morning return since I worked faithfully whether I was being observed or not. Likewise, when we abide in Jesus, we can go through life boldly and not have to worry about the timing of His imminent return.

My treasured brother or sister in Christ, I exhort you to intentionally reside in Jesus all the day long, so that you can be ready to have a freedom of dialogue with Him when He appears. Start your day in the Word and prayer, and allow that Word to be thought about throughout the day as you talk to God. God created you to fellowship with Him; fulfill your God-given design and rejoice as your await His blessed return.

Our next employment point from 1 John 2:29: *Imitate Jesus' righteousness, revealing that you are born again.* Heed John's words from 1 John 3:7, "Little children, let no one deceive you, He who practices righteousness is righteous, just as He is righteous." When we openly identify with Jesus, the world watches us.

I want you to memorize Matthew 5:6 to help you fulfill this assignment and to reflect Jesus in your life: "Blessed are those who hunger and thirst for righteousness, for they shall be filled." Write that verse on your heart and crave that which really satisfies: Jesus' righteousness. Then, model that you are saved by that pursuit.

Our third employment point is a major game changer: *Hope in Jesus' return for purified living* (1 John 3:1–3). Going back to the Beatitudes, Matthew 5:8 declares, "Blessed are the pure in heart, for they shall see God." Living in light of Jesus' imminent return will clean up your life so that you can see God more clearly. We are pilgrims in this life and shouldn't be enamored by what this world has to offer, since our citizenship lies in heaven.

May I encourage you to apply this third and vital application point with a weekly fast, lasting one month? Please abstain from a particular meal, or from watching a daily program like the news, and replace it with a concentrated time of prayer and reading the Word, asking Jesus to keep you vigilantly awaiting His return. You will want to write out 1 John 2:28–3:3 and review it weekly during this time of focused worship.

CHAPTER TEN

WHO IS HEAD OF YOUR FAMILY TREE?

1 JOHN 3:4–10

—⁓⁓—

A man wasn't feeling well, so he went to his doctor for a complete checkup. After a long wait for the results, the doctor finally came back out. He said, "I'm afraid I have some very bad news. You're dying, and you don't have much time left."

"Oh no! I can't believe it!" says the man. "How long do I have?"

"Ten," the doctor says sadly.

"Ten?" the man asks. "What do you mean by that? Ten what? Months? Weeks? What?"

The doctor then said, "Nine."

This man was just "nine" away from meeting the head of his family tree. As Christians, *Jesus* is the head of our tree—or vine, if you prefer (see John 15). Therefore, John now transitions from abiding in Christ, as we await the rapture, to abstaining from sin based upon Jesus' first coming. As always, let us reverently read our text:

> Whoever commits sin also commits lawlessness, and sin is lawlessness. And you know that He was manifested to take away our sins, and in Him there is no sin. Whoever abides in Him does not sin. Whoever sins has neither seen Him nor known Him.
>
> Little children, let no one deceive you. He who practices righteousness is righteous, just as He is righteous. He who sins is of the devil, for the devil has sinned from the beginning. For this purpose the Son of God was manifested, that He might destroy the works of the devil. Whoever has been born of God does not sin, for His

seed remains in him; and he cannot sin, because he has been born of God.

In this the children of God and the children of the devil are manifest: Whoever does not practice righteousness is not of God, nor *is* he who does not love his brother (1 John 3:4–10).

Everyone who sins breaks the law; in fact, sin is lawlessness. But you know that he appeared so that he might take away our sins. And in him is no sin. No one who lives in him keeps on sinning. No one who continues to sin has either seen him or known him. Dear children, do not let anyone lead you astray. He who does what is right is righteous, just as he is righteous. He who does what is sinful is of the devil, because the devil has been sinning from the beginning. The reason the Son of God appeared was to destroy the devil's work. No one who is born of God will continue to sin, because God's seed remains in him; he cannot go on sinning, because he has been born of God. This is how we know who the children of God are and who the children of the devil are: Anyone who does not do what is right is not a child of God; nor is anyone who does not love his brother (1 John 3:4–10, NIV 84).

THE SIMULTANEOUS PURSUIT OF ABIDING AND ABSTAINING—F

- Why does John point to Jesus being sinless in 1 John 3:5?
- Does one act of sin mean you've "neither seen Him nor known Him" (1 John 3:6)?
- Does one sinful act mean you are "of the devil" (1 John 3:8)?
- What does it mean that Jesus "was manifested that He might destroy the works of the devil," in 1 John 3:8?
- Does the born-again saint never sin, and cannot sin, according to 1 John 3:9?

THE SIMULTANEOUS PURSUIT OF
ABIDING AND ABSTAINING—I

Before attending the Washington Bible College and Capital Bible Seminary, I taught myself Greek. First John became the first book of the Greek New Testament that I translated approximately thirty-years ago. I had many Greek courses over the next twenty years, and I'm so glad for what I've learned so that I can give some much needed clarification concerning the passage before us. This is one of those paragraphs where the Greek language gives pertinent insight.

There are numerous present tense verbs in our passage, showing continuous action in present time. "Commits sin" becomes the first one in our paragraph, when John writes in 1 John 3:4, "Whoever commits sin also commits lawlessness." John equates "sin," which means "missing the mark," with "lawlessness," which derives from the alpha privative designating negation, and the Greek root, which carries the meaning of law. The literal denotation is "without the law." To habitually practice sin is to remain in a state of lawlessness.

Next, John states the intent for Jesus' first coming, "And you know that He was manifested to take away our sins" (1 John 3:5). Our Lord's first advent had the express purpose to make Him visible or apparent (the meaning of the Greek word translated "manifest") so that He could take up or lift up (the thrust of the term "take away") our sins. Furthermore, John pens why our Lord could do this: "and in Him there is no sin." The literal Greek word order translates, "and sin in Him is not." The verb "is" occurs in the present tense, which shows that Jesus' eternal nature is sinless.

The apostle of love then draws a correlation in 1 John 3:6, "Whoever abides in Him does not sin." "Abides" appears as a present participle, and "sins" also occurs in the present tense. John's meaning: When the child of God resides in Christ as a way of life, then he or she cannot continually sin.

John resumes in 1 John 3:6, "Whoever sins has neither seen Him nor known Him." This time John uses the present participle for "sins," again demonstrating how one lives, and two perfect tense verbs ("seen" and "known"), which speak of a completed action in the past with the results continuing. John declares that the individual who misses God's standards habitually does not have a relationship with the Lord, and never did.

John then warned his flock from 1 John 3:7 with a present tense command prefaced by his fatherly affection, "Little children, let no one deceive you." As a vigilant overseer, he knew that the false teachers were currently lurking in the vicinity, with their desire to lead the sheep astray. With the second half of the verse he reminds them, "He who practices righteousness is righteous," and uses Jesus as the perfect measuring rod, "just as He is righteous."

If the person who sins continually doesn't know the Lord according to 1 John 3:6, to whom does that individual belong? Who is the head of his or her family tree? First John 3:8 answers those questions, "He who sins is of the devil." Once again John makes use of the present participle, to connect consistent sinful activity with belonging to Satan. The prince of darkness "has sinned from the beginning." Since Satan fell from heaven, he has maintained that sinful posture as demonstrated in Genesis 3, just like the man or woman who never has been regenerated (born again).

John next states another motivation for Jesus' first coming: "For this purpose the Son of God was manifested, that He might destroy the works of the devil." The apostle strategically used the past tense verb "destroy" to show that Christ's death loosed or untied (the meaning of the Greek verb translated "destroy") the wicked one's works through His death, as explained in 1 John 3:5.

This tightly woven paragraph continues in 1 John 3:9, "Whoever has been born of God does not sin." Those who have been born of God (past) with the results continuing (shown by the perfect passive verb "born") cannot sin habitually (taught by the present tense verb "does"). The reason: They have been implanted with a new capacity to overcome sin via the Holy Spirit. Therefore John argues, "His seed remains in him; and he cannot sin, because he has been born of God." The "seed" refers to the new nature as an outcome of the indwelling Holy Spirit; as a result, "he cannot sin" continually.

John culminates this masterfully written paragraph with, "In this the children of God and the children of the devil are manifest: Whoever does not practice righteousness is not of God, nor *is* he who does not love his brother" (1 John 3:10). Simply stated: You model that you are born again if you regularly live righteously and continually direct your will to love your brother. Conversely, you are not saved if you regularly practice unrighteousness, and as a manner of life hate people.

John gives some stark contrasts between the just and unjust. Let's trace these concepts throughout Scripture to see their relationship with his text.

THE SIMULTANEOUS PURSUIT OF ABIDING AND ABSTAINING—R

Back in 1 John 2:1 we studied that John didn't want his flock to sin. He recorded, "My little children, these things I write to you, that you may not sin." John elaborates upon the vile nature of sin with a comparison in 1 John 3:4, "Whoever commits sin also commits lawlessness, and sin is lawlessness." The Greek term for "lawlessness" appears fifteen times in the Greek New Testament. It first occurs in Matthew 7:23 where Jesus assesses those who pretended to be His children, and were not, and characterized them as follows, "I never knew you; depart from Me, you who practice lawlessness." Sin and lawlessness aptly depict the unsaved and Satan; however, the children of God shouldn't display these ungodly traits.

Satan's present emissaries the antichrists, and his future liaison the Antichrist, all exude lawlessness. Consider 2 Thessalonians 2:7–8a: "For the mystery of lawlessness is already at work; only He [the Holy Spirit] who now restrains *will do so* until He is taken out of the way. And then the lawless one will be revealed." God's Holy Spirit thwarts the Antichrist from appearing, and the Spirit will be removed in the rapture before the Antichrist's future manifestation. Although the Holy Spirit will still be in operation during the tribulation, His presence will be removed in part because believers who have the Spirit within will have been caught up to heaven.

Since "the mystery of lawlessness" was operational 2,000 years ago, John wrote the saints at Ephesus to stay clear of the false teachers because of their lawbreaking ways. Paul, who defended his apostleship in 2 Corinthians, warned the saints at Corinth not to mingle with these ambassadors for

Satan. "Do not be unequally yoked together with unbelievers," argued the apostle to the Gentiles in 2 Corinthians 6:14, "For what fellowship has righteousness with lawlessness? And what communion has light with darkness?"

Jesus came "to take away our sins," according to 1 John 3:5. Because of His sinless nature, "the Son of God was manifested, that He might destroy the works of the devil" (1 John 3:8). John goes on to connect the dots: "He who sins [continually] is of the devil, for the devil has sinned from the beginning." Before we explore the fall of Satan, our longing should consist of glorifying God by abstaining from sin, which is lawlessness, and to glorify the Father by not imitating the one who "sinned from the beginning."

The sixth-century BC prophet Ezekiel addresses "the prince of Tyre," and chides him for his pride in Ezekiel 28:2: "Because your heart is lifted up, And you say, 'I am a god, I sit *in* the seat of gods, In the midst of the seas,' Yet you are a man, and not a god, though you set your heart as the heart of a god." Ezekiel then uses the connecting planks of pride and discontentment to build a bridge to Satan, which happens in Ezekiel 28:11–12, "Moreover the word of the LORD came to me saying, 'Son of man, take up a lamentation for the king of Tyre.'" Did you notice that previously Ezekiel 28:2 speaks about "the prince of Tyre," while Ezekiel 28:12" focuses upon "the king of Tyre"? Furthermore, Ezekiel writes, "You were the seal of perfection, full of wisdom and perfect in beauty. You were in Eden, the garden of God" (Ezek. 28:12b–13a). Clearly he was no longer talking about a man, since "You were in Eden, the garden of God."

Observe how the prince of darkness had enjoyed the supreme privilege of serving God in heaven as an "anointed cherub" (cherubim being angels designated to guard God's holiness). Note also his subsequent betrayal in Ezekiel 28:14–15, "You were the anointed cherub who covers; I established you; you were on the holy mountain of God; you walked back and forth in the midst of fiery stones. You were perfect [blameless or complete] in your ways from the day you were created, till iniquity was found in you."

Satan, who was created by God, became unjust (the meaning of the Hebrew word for "iniquity"). Because of his departure from doing what was right, God expelled him from heaven; the devil personifies lawlessness. Jesus came to undo the lawless one's deeds. Since Jesus' finished work sets us free, we are no longer to imitate Satan, but rather to abide in Christ in order not to submit to sin, which is lawlessness.

Having gained a better understanding of this profound text, let's see what we need to abide in, and abstain from, according to 1 John 3:4–10.

THE SIMULTANEOUS PURSUIT OF ABIDING AND ABSTAINING—E

Our passage had many present tense verbs, showing continuous action in present time. Please regard the two employment points as both also in the present tense. In other words, linear action is what our text demands.

Abide in the sinless Jesus to overcome sin is employment point number one, based upon 1 John 3:4–6. In 2 Corinthians 5:21, Paul trumpets how Jesus, the perfect sacrifice, emancipated us from Satan's grip, "For He [God] made Him [Jesus] who knew no sin to be sin for us, that we might become the righteousness of God in Him." The sinless Jesus became our substitute and took our lawlessness upon Himself, so that we could be liberated from Satan's clutches and have victory over sin.

The passport not to sin is to consistently abide in Jesus. We've seen in our previous paragraph (1 John 2:28–3:3) that abiding in Christ will keep us prepared for an open conversation with Jesus when He returns. Similarly, residing in our Lord keeps us daily from falling prey to Satan's method of tempting us by the lust of the flesh, the lust of the eyes, and the pride of life. Abide in Jesus, amigo, so that you don't sin.

The second linear practice also begins with the letter "a": *Abstain from sin to display your new birth*, which derives from 1 John 3:7–10. John pulled no punches; whatever we consistently do shows to whom we belong. "Little children, let no one deceive you. He who practices righteousness is righteous, just as He is righteous. He who sins is of the devil" (1 John 3:7–8a). Clearly the apostle desired his little children to shun lawless activities to display that they've been born again.

How does the child of God abstain from sin to showcase his or her new capacity—as a result of the indwelling Holy Spirit—not to practice unrighteousness? He needs to *abide in the sinless Jesus to overcome sin*. The first application point was stated positively. Our second employment point appears negatively; *abstain from sin to display your new birth*. As we herald that we don't belong to Satan, let's make sure that we portray our God well by residing in Him.

CHAPTER ELEVEN

GENUINE LOVE MEETS NEEDS
1 JOHN 3:11–18

⸻〰⸺

A despondent woman was walking along the beach, when she saw a bottle on the sand. She picked it up and pulled out the cork. Whoosh! A big puff of smoke appeared. The genie told her, "You've released me from prison. To show my thanks, I will grant you three wishes. But take care, for with each wish, your mate will receive double of whatever you request."

"Why?" The woman asked. "That bum left me for another woman."

The genie replied, "That is how it is written."

The woman shrugged and then asked for a million dollars. There was a flash of light, and a million dollars appeared at her feet. At the same instant, in a far-off place, her wayward husband looked down and saw twice that amount at his feet. "And your second wish?"

"Genie, I want the world's most expensive diamond necklace." Another flash of light, and the woman was holding the precious treasure. And in a distant place, her husband was now holding a massive gem.

"Genie, is it really true that my husband has two million dollars and more jewels than I do, and that he gets double of whatever I wish for?"

The genie said, "It is indeed true."

"Okay genie, I'm ready for my last wish," the woman said. "Scare me half to death!"

I don't believe that this peeved woman had her husband's best interest in mind, particularly with her third wish. The apostle of love had just instructed his flock that they should be practicing righteousness and enjoying victory over sin. John now also has three wishes in the text before us. He desires that all of us understand this triad about genuine Christian love from 1 John 3:11–18:

For this is the message that you heard from the beginning, that we should love one another, not as Cain *who* was of the wicked one and murdered his brother. And why did he murder him? Because his works were evil and his brother's righteous.

Do not marvel, my brethren, if the world hates you. We know that we have passed from death to life, because we love the brethren. He who does not love *his* brother abides in death. Whoever hates his brother is a murderer, and you know that no murderer has eternal life abiding in him.

By this we know love, because He laid down His life for us. And we also ought to lay down *our* lives for the brethren. But whoever has this world's goods, and sees his brother in need, and shuts up his heart from him, how does the love of God abide in him?

My little children, let us not love in word or in tongue, but in deed and in truth (1 John 3:11–18).

For this is the message which you have heard from the beginning, that we should love one another; not as Cain, *who* was of the evil one and slew his brother. And for what reason did he slay him? Because his deeds were evil, and his brother's were righteous.

Do not be surprised, brethren, if the world hates you. We know that we have passed out of death into life, because we love the brethren. He who does not love abides in death. Everyone who hates his brother is a murderer; and you know that no murderer has eternal life abiding in him. We know love by this, that He laid down His life for us; and we ought to lay down our lives for the brethren. But whoever has the world's goods, and sees his brother in need and closes his heart against him, how does the love of God abide in him? Little children, let us not love with word or with tongue, but in deed and truth (1 John 3:11–18, NASB).

JOHN'S THREE WISHES FOR YOU—F

- Who does the "one another" refer to in 1 John 3:11?

- Why does John use Cain as an example in 1 John 3:12?
- In particular, why does the world hate the saints, based on 1 John 3:13?
- Who is the "brother" in 1 John 3:15?
- Why does John change from the plural "brethren" in 1 John 3:16 to the singular "brother" in 1 John 3:17?

JOHN'S THREE WISHES FOR YOU—I

John begins this passage with an expression similar to one he used back in 1 John 1:5, "This is the message which we have heard from Him" with that introduction, he reminded the believers "that God is light." Now in 1 John 3:11, he states our obligation to each other, "For this is the message that you heard from the beginning, that we should love one another."

After exhorting the saints to "love one another," why does John then use Cain as a negative example? Since the apostle had just encouraged the body of Christ to love their brothers and sisters, Cain was a suitable example of one who didn't love his brother, Abel. The elder brother revealed his perverse heart, and that he belonged to Satan, by his actions. That's the reason John pens, "not as Cain who was of the wicked one and murdered his brother. And why did he murder him? Because his works were evil and his brother's righteous" (1 John 3:12).

Smoothly and perceptively, the apostle makes the connection between Cain's evil deeds and Abel's righteous works: "Do not marvel, my brethren, if the world hates you" (1 John 3:13). The present imperative "do not marvel" conveys the concept "stop marveling." In essence, children of God shouldn't be astonished when this world's system opposes the righteous works of believers, because from the beginning Satan has sought to silence his foes.

John then shifts gears with the emphatic "we know" in 1 John 3:14. What is it that the saints know intuitively? First, it is stated positively, "We know that we have passed from death to life because we love the brethren." God's proof-of-purchase seal on our lives makes a public showing through our visible love toward one another. He then states negatively in the same verse, "He who does not love his brother abides in death." The two present tense verbs ("love" and "abides") communicate that a habitual absence of love for the saints reveals a person who remains spiritually dead.

The sagacious apostle then links hatred to murder in 1 John 3:15, "Whoever hates his brother is a murderer." The present participle "hates" indicates a deep residing animosity toward an individual. Another nexus then occurs in our verse, "and you know that no murderer has eternal life abiding in him." To sum up 1 John 3:15: A consistent hatred of another human being equals murder, and a murderer in heart cannot be a genuine believer.

If hatred of our fellow man reveals a murderer at heart, what characteristic displays a saved heart? "By this we know love," wrote John, "because He laid down His life for us" (1 John 3:16). The first half of this verse reminds us of God's demonstrated love for the world from John 3:16. But the second half of this verse shows the other side of the coin, "And we also ought to lay down our lives for the brethren." Jesus' one-time act, as displayed by the past tense verb "laid down," becomes our present pattern of obligation ("we ought to") for us to "lay down" our bodies, if necessary, in behalf of our brothers and sisters in Christ.

In 1 John 3:16, John uses the plural "brethren." Observe his change to the singular in 1 John 3:17, "But whoever has this world's goods, and sees his brother in need, and shuts up his heart from him, how does the love of God abide in Him?" Why did John do this? C. S. Lewis perhaps answered this best when he wrote, "Loving everybody in general may be an excuse for loving nobody in particular." To not show compassion to a child of God in need makes one question whether God's love resides in that individual.

John closes out the paragraph with an appropriate call to action, "My little children, let us not love in word or in tongue, but in deed and in truth" (1 John 3:18). Lip service isn't satisfactory to the apostle of love; he requires a response of compassion calling for a Christ-like love that meets the needs of others. The rest of Scripture has much to say on this worthy topic.

JOHN'S THREE WISHES FOR YOU—R

The "apostle of love" received his designation because he practiced what

Jesus had preached. After Jesus washed the feet of His disciples, including John, He said, "By this all will know that you are My disciples, if you have love for one another" (John 13:35). John received the baton from His beloved Master and then passed it to the next generation, "For this is the message that you heard from the beginning, that we should love one another" (1 John 3:11). Whether it was Jesus, John, or the writer of Hebrews, the exhortation remains the same, "Let brotherly love continue" (Heb. 13:1).

Our paragraph feels like you are watching a tennis match, with love on one side of the court and hate on the other. John makes a fascinating association about the hate side of the court in 1 John 3:15, "Whoever hates his brother is a murderer." Decades prior Jesus—in the greatest sermon ever preached, the Sermon on the Mount—made a similar connection: "You have heard that it was said to those of old, 'You shall not murder,' and whoever murders will be in danger of the judgment. But I say to you that whoever is angry with his brother, without a cause shall be in danger of the judgment" (Matt. 5:21–22a).

Jesus and John both exposed that Cain was a murderer even before he killed his brother. No wonder that the writer of Proverbs gave the following nugget of wisdom: "Keep your heart with all diligence, for out of it *spring* the issues of life" (Prov. 4:23). The Hebrew word for "keep" carries the idea to carefully protect what has been entrusted to you. Protect your hearts, my beloved brethren.

Let's allow our necks to turn back toward the love side of the tennis court. John wrote, "By this we know love, because He laid down His life for us. And we also ought to lay down our lives for the brethren" (1 John 3:16). Again, John learned well from Jesus, who said, "Greater love has no one than this, than to lay down one's life for his friends" (John 15:13). Our Lord literally did this; we are called to be ready to do the same.

In the meantime, how do we demonstrate that we love our brothers and sisters, since most of us will never be called upon to offer our physical lives for another? Sharing our time and money for our church family in need demonstrates our genuine love. John queried, "But whoever has this world's goods, and sees his brother in need, and shuts up his heart from him, how does the love of God abide in Him?" (1 John 3:17).

Moreover, John despised mere lip service when it came to meeting needs. For this reason he penned, "My little children, let us not love in word or in tongue, but in deed and in truth" (1 John 3:18). James concurred, "If a brother or sister is naked and destitute of daily food, and one of you says to them, 'Depart in peace, be warmed and filled,' but you do not give them the things which are needed for the body, what does it profit?" (James 2:16). Both John and James offered stinging questions—particularly to those who weren't applying these biblical principles.

Speaking about application and principles, I'm chomping at the bit to move on to employment, based upon what we've just studied. Lace up your work boots, my friends; it's time to go to work.

JOHN'S THREE WISHES FOR YOU—E

What are John's three aspirations for you? *Love one another continually to display God's love* becomes employment point one from 1 John 3:11–13. Although the apostle of love drew the congregation's attention to the fact that this world will hate them, he also shared, "For this is the message that you heard from the beginning, that we should love one another" (1 John 3:11).

As a pastor, I've performed many wedding ceremonies. Prior to a couple taking their vows, I generally meet with them over the course of several months to give premarital counseling. One portion of Scripture I always have them memorize is 1 Corinthians 13:4–8a. Your first assignment consists of memorizing, and more importantly, internalizing these verses: "Love suffers long *and is* kind; love does not envy; love does not parade itself, is not puffed up; does not behave rudely, does not seek its own, is not provoked, thinks no evil; does not rejoice in iniquity, but rejoices in the truth; bears all things, believes all things, hopes all things, endures all things. Love never fails" (1 Cor. 13:4–8a). Consider how these verses can begin to flow from your heart to those around you.

Your second employment point is as follows: *Love one another continually to display your salvation*, which derives from 1 John 3:14–15. How can the unsaved witness God's redeeming power in us? Consider 1 John 3:14: "We know that we have passed from death to life because we love the brethren." Not only does your continual *agape* love reassure your heart that you are born again, but also it permits the lost to see a display of His amazing grace.

No one's love ever measured up to Jesus' love for His own. Just before washing the apostles' feet and going to the cross, John recorded the extent of our Lord's love. He wrote in John 13:1, "having loved His own who were in the world, He loved them to the end." The idea of the text just isn't that Jesus loved His disciples until His last moment on planet earth, but that He loved them fully with all of His holy being. Hence, I want you to commit to the Almighty to pursue the teaching of Hebrews 13:1, which says, "Let brotherly love continue." Imitate Jesus here, my extended family, and let the world marvel at your transformed existence.

John's third ambition for us occurs in our third employment point, from 1 John 3:16–18: *Love one another continually to display Jesus' sacrifice.* As you meet the needs of your brothers and sisters in Christ, extend your hand and give them the help that they need, both physical and spiritual, to advance them to the place where they can bless others.

The church of Jesus Christ was birthed during a time of poverty in Acts 2. How did the saints respond who had the means to give a hand up? "Now the multitude of those who believed were of one heart and one soul; neither did anyone say that any of the things he possessed was his own, but they had all things in common," wrote Luke in Acts 4:32. "Nor was there anyone among them who lacked; for all who were possessors of lands or houses sold them, and brought the proceeds of the things that were sold, and laid *them* at the apostles' feet; and they distributed to each as anyone had need" (Acts 4:34–35).

This sacrificial example of love by the early church testified to the strong belief that Jesus had given His life for them and they were in return to give their lives for each other. That's why John could ask, "But whoever has this world's goods, and sees his brother in need, and shuts up his heart from him, how does the love of God abide in Him?" (1 John 3:17). Our God gave us His best by sending His only begotten Son; subsequently, the Son gave us His all by dying for you and me. Shall we not also be ready to lay down our lives for our brothers and sisters through surrendering those things we can't take with us, to supply what our Christian family needs right now?

CHAPTER TWELVE

FREEDOM OF SPEECH TOWARD GOD

1 JOHN 3:19–24

—∿∿∾—

A Sunday School teacher read selected verses from the Old Testament book of Jonah to her class: "Now the LORD had prepared a great fish to swallow Jonah. And Jonah was in the belly of the fish three days and three nights. Then Jonah prayed to the LORD his God from the fish's belly. And he said: 'I cried out to the LORD because of my affliction, and he answered me.' So the LORD spoke to the fish, and it vomited Jonah onto dry *land*" (Jonah 1:17–2:2; 2:10).

When she had finished reading, the teacher said, "Now, children, you have heard the Bible story of Jonah and the big fish. What does the story teach us?" A ten-year-old student shouted out: "You can't keep a good man down!"

Some good men might feel that they are being kept down because their hearts are troubling them. John gives great advice on how to overcome being kept down, in 1 John 3:19–24:

> And by this we know that we are of the truth, and shall assure our hearts before Him. For if our heart condemns us, God is greater than our heart, and knows all things. Beloved, if our heart does not condemn us, we have confidence toward God. And whatever we ask we receive from Him, because we keep His commandments and do those things that are pleasing in His sight. And this is His commandment: that we should believe on the name of His Son Jesus Christ and love one another, as He gave us commandment.
>
> Now he who keeps His commandments abides in Him, and He in him. And by this we know that He abides in us, by the Spirit whom He has given us (1 John 3:19–24).

And by this we will know that we are of the truth and will convince our conscience in his presence, that if our conscience condemns us, that God is greater than our conscience and knows all things. Dear friends, if our conscience does not condemn us, we have confidence in the presence of God, and whatever we ask we receive from him, because we keep his commandments and do the things that are pleasing to him. Now this is his commandment: that we believe in the name of his Son Jesus Christ and love one another, just as he gave us the commandment. And the person who keeps his commandments resides in God, and God in him. Now by this we know that God resides in us: by the Spirit he has given us (1 John 3:19–24, NET).

THREE PERKS OF LOVING YOUR BRETHREN—F

- What do the words "by this" refer to in 1 John 3:19?
- How do we know if we can trust our hearts, according to 1 John 3:19–20?
- Is the Greek word for "confidence" in 1 John 3:21 the same one used in 1 John 2:28?
- To what extent should we take the assertion in 1 John 3:22, that "whatever we ask we receive from Him because we keep His commandments?"
- What is the relationship between abiding and the Holy Spirit, from 1 John 3:24?

THREE PERKS OF LOVING YOUR BRETHREN—I

John begins our new paragraph, "And by this we know that we are of the truth, and shall assure our hearts before Him" (1 John 3:19). The "heart" is the seat of personality, and "by this" points back to 1 John 3:14 and 16–17. John demonstrates a bond between loving the brethren and experientially knowing "that we are of the truth." Sometimes believers need to assure, persuade, or appease their hearts that they are of the truth because their hearts accuse them unjustly.

The apostle continues, "For if our heart condemns us, God is greater than our heart, and knows all things" (1 John 3:20). We will study, under relationship, why our hearts are not trustworthy. Let it suffice to say here that God has better discernment than our hearts, and that we can trust Him fully even when our hearts have duped us. Our actions, loving our brothers and sisters in Christ, trump any false message that our hearts may convey.

It is clear that if we don't have a confidence toward God because our hearts condemn us, we won't boldly approach His throne. Conversely, according to 1 John 3:21, "Beloved, if our heart does not condemn us, we have confidence toward God." We studied the word "confidence" earlier in 1 John 2:28, which literally means "all speech." Not only does the child of God need to have a freedom of speech when he appears before the judgment seat of Christ, but he or she also needs it now to seek the Father's spiritual and physical provision through prayer.

Once we have freedom of discourse with our heavenly Father, then "whatever we ask we receive from Him, because we keep His commandments and do those things that are pleasing in His sight" (1 John 3:22). The verb "we ask" refers to the request from an inferior to a superior. The idea is that, as we abide in Christ, we will be asking for those things that are pleasing to Him.

Moreover, God delights to honor His children with answers to prayer when we obey His Word, and continually strive to have lives that bring the Lord satisfaction. Both verbs from verse 22, "we keep" and "do," are in the present tense, which show that when we are guarding His commandments, and are doing the activities that are pleasant in His presence, He honors our petitions.

Before you can abide in Jesus, you need to believe in Him. That is the order presented in 1 John 3:23–24. Let's first observe verse 23, "And this is His commandment: that we should believe on the name of His Son Jesus Christ and love one another, as He gave us commandment." John takes the plural "His commandments" from verse 22 and reduces them to one "commandment" in verse 23. John shows that one side of the coin is to believe in Jesus, while the other side is to love one another. This is the first of ten occurrences in our epistle where John uses the verb "believe," When someone places their reliance upon Jesus for salvation, that changed life should become known to all onlookers because of the demonstration of love toward the body of Christ.

There should come a mutual abiding after placing one's faith in Jesus. John writes, "Now he who keeps His commandments abides in Him, and He in Him" (1 John 3:24a). Again John uses the present tense verb "abides," to draw the readers' attention to a continual state of residing in Jesus. The benefits of mutual abiding are out of this world; not only do we get to walk with Jesus, but He also resides with us.

How are we to be aware that this mutual abiding takes place? "And by this we know that He abides in us, by the Spirit whom He has given us" (1 John 3:24b). For the first time in our epistle John used the term "Spirit." This very same Spirit gives the inner witness to us being in Jesus, and Him being in us.

Let me give you the second half of 1 John 3:24, translated word-by-word from the Greek: "And in/by this we are experientially knowing that He is abiding in us, from the Spirit whom to us was given." This first occurrence of "Spirit" in our epistle is key to interpreting 1 John 4:1–6; however, we need to first finish *this* chapter, before probing further into the Spirit's ministry in the next chapter.

THREE PERKS OF LOVING YOUR BRETHREN—R

How can our hearts trick us? Jeremiah answered that question and asked another in Jeremiah 17:9. He revealed and pondered, "The heart *is* deceitful above all *things*, and desperately wicked; who can know it?" The Hebrew word translated "desperately wicked" here is rendered "incurable" in Jeremiah 15:18 and 30:12. The general meaning is "to be sick." The human heart carries the inherited disease known as sin sickness; this is why it cannot be relied upon fully.

David, the sweet psalmist of Israel, a man after God's own heart, wrote about himself, "Behold, I was brought forth in iniquity, and in sin my mother conceived me" (Ps. 51:5). One thousand years after David made that proclamation about the sin nature, Jesus gave another: "For out of the heart proceed evil thoughts, murders, adulteries, fornications, thefts, false witness, blasphemies" (Matt. 15:19).

Satan regularly hurls indictments against the saints; he revels in condemning the just. The apostle John, when banished on the island of Patmos, wrote about Satan's future permanent expulsion from heaven during the tribulation. Revelation 12:10 reports, "for the accuser of our brethren, who accused them before our God day and night, has been cast down." Between living with a fallen condition that has impaired men's hearts for millennia, and the incessant attacks from the wicked one, it is no wonder that our hearts can erroneously judge us.

For these reasons the child of God, although enjoying the indwelling presence of the Holy Spirit, needs to be aware that his heart can condemn him unjustly. Where should we turn in times of doubt? John tenderly addressed this matter, "Beloved, if our heart condemns us, God is greater than our heart, and knows all things" (1 John 3:21). Child of God, when you need to call the status of your heart into question, make your appeal to the all-knowing God.

The writer of Proverbs wisely cautioned, "He who trusts in his own heart is a fool" (Prov. 28:26). Since that is the case, let's then turn to the One who created our souls, which includes our hearts, and knows everything about us.

We already have the diagnosis of the heart's incurably sick condition from Dr. Jeremiah, the cardiologist, in Jeremiah 17:9. In the next verse, he becomes Dr. Jeremiah the ophthalmologist, and gives us heavenly glasses to refocus our vision: "I, the LORD, search the heart, I test the mind, Even to give every man according to his ways, And according to the fruit of his doings" (Jer. 17:10). Jeremiah and John essentially say the same thing; God possesses knowledge superior to what's in our hearts, so let's turn to Him in times of skepticism.

Once God corrects our erring hearts, then "we have confidence toward God." Not only that, "And whatever we ask we receive from Him, because we keep His commandments and do those things that are pleasing in His sight" (1 John 3:22). Turn to the all-knowing One to search your heart, and just stay focused upon obeying His Word and pleasing Him always.

THREE PERKS OF LOVING YOUR BRETHREN—E

What are the three perks of loving your brethren? Fringe benefit number one: *Love your brother and experience assurance of salvation* (1 John 3:19–20). As we've just studied, our hearts at times can trick us and lead us awry. On account of this John guides his flock, "And by this we know that we are of the truth, and shall assure of our hearts before Him" (1 John 3:19). The "by this" refers back to 1 John 3:14 and 16–17 and concerns loving our church family.

One safeguard to affirm that you are saved is to love God's children. Our example for this paradigm was Jesus: "By this we know love, because He laid down His life for us. And we also ought to lay down *our* lives for the brethren" (1 John 3:16). James 1:8 informs us, "a double-minded [literally "double-souled"] man is unstable in all his ways." Your employment here consists of evaluating whether you are regularly serving and meeting the needs of the saints. If not, schedule a meeting with your pastor or a church leader who can give you opportunities to practice this application point.

Has God been regularly answering your prayers? The implementation or non-compliance with our second employment point—*love your brother and experience answered prayer* (from 1 John 3:21–22)—might reveal why you have responded to that question either affirmatively or negatively. John imparts a tremendous incentive to act upon the knowledge you've just received: "And whatever we ask we receive from Him, because we keep His commandments and do those things that are pleasing in His sight" (1 John 3:22).

Do you ever wonder how many answers to prayer Jesus experienced while upon the earth? I'm sure He knew what to pray for because of His close relationship with the Father. His daily "conference calls" helped focus Him perfectly toward the will of God. He could confidently offer, "And He who sent Me is with Me. The Father has not left Me alone, for I always do those things that please Him" (John 8:29).

Since we are to love God with all of our being, and we demonstrate that we love Him by caring deeply for our brothers and sisters in Christ, we need to both maintain a steady diet of good works serving the Christian community and to strive to pray as Jesus did. The end result will be a greatly benefited body of believers because of your love for them and many answers to prayer.

Our third perk is equally impressive, and is based upon 1 John 3:23–24: *Love your brother and experience abiding in Christ.* John simply stated it as follows: "Now he who keeps His commandment abides in Him" (1 John 3:24). In the gospel of John 13–15, Jesus spoke often to His disciples about keeping the Father's commandments by loving one another and abiding in Him. What's the end result of residing in Jesus? "Abide in Me, and I in you. As the branch cannot bear fruit of itself, unless it abides in the vine, neither can you, unless you abide in Me" (John 15:4).

My beloved brother or sister, love God's family as Jesus did. The triad of benefits from experiencing assurance of salvation, answered prayer, and abiding in Christ make any competing offer this temporal world has to give pale in comparison.

CHAPTER THIRTEEN

EXPOSING THE
FALSE PROPHET'S MESSAGE

1 JOHN 4:1–6

⎯⌇⌇⎯

On the road one day, a man and a woman smashed their cars together in a terrible car wreck. Both vehicles were totaled, but fortunately neither person was injured. The woman said to the man, "Thank goodness we're both okay! We should celebrate. I have a bottle of wine in my car, so let's open it and toast the fact that we survived the wreck."

The man agreed and the woman opened the bottle of wine and handed it to him. He took a huge swallow and handed it back. The woman closed the bottle and set it down by his car. The man asked, "Aren't you going to take a drink?"

"No," the woman said. "I think I'll just wait for the cops to get here."

Deception rears its ugly head all around us. But how can we know when someone is trying to deceive us concerning spiritual matters? In our last chapter, we saw that the Holy Spirit enables believers to know that Christ abides in us. The same Holy Spirit also equips us to decipher the message of false prophets who are energized by deceiving spirits.

Thank God for giving us His revelation to help us discern truth from lies. Allow His holy Word to permeate your soul as we prayerfully read 1 John 4:1–6:

> Beloved, do not believe every spirit, but test the spirits, whether they are of God; because many false prophets have gone out into the world. By this you know the Spirit of God: Every spirit that confesses that Jesus Christ has come in the flesh is of God, and every spirit that does not confess that Jesus Christ has come in

the flesh is not of God. And this is the *spirit* of the Antichrist, which you have heard was coming, and is now already in the world.

You are of God, little children, and have overcome them, because He who is in you is greater than he who is in the world. They are of the world. Therefore they speak *as* of the world, and the world hears them. We are of God. He who knows God hears us; he who is not of God does not hear us. By this we know the spirit of truth and the spirit of error (1 John 4:1–6).

Dear friends, don't believe everyone who claims to have the Spirit of God. Test them all to find out if they really do come from God. Many false prophets have already gone out into the world, and you can know which ones come from God. His Spirit says that Jesus Christ had a truly human body. But when someone doesn't say this about Jesus, you know that person has a spirit that doesn't come from God and is the enemy of Christ. You knew that this enemy was coming into the world and now is already here.

Children, you belong to God, and you have defeated these enemies. God's Spirit is in you and is more powerful than the one that is in the world. These enemies belong to this world, and the world listens to them, because they speak its language. We belong to God, and everyone who knows God will listen to us. But the people who don't know God won't listen to us. That is how we can tell the Spirit that speaks the truth from the one that tells lies (1 John 4:1–6, CEV).

SIZE UP A SPIRIT BY THE SWORD AND "THE" SPIRIT—F

- How do you test "the spirits," as referenced in 1 John 4:1?
- How can a spirit confess "that Jesus Christ has come in the flesh," according to 1 John 4:2?
- Who does the "them" point to in the expression "and have overcome them" in 1 John 4:4?

- When 1 John 4:6 reports, "We are of God... He who knows God hears us," who does the "we" and "us" refer to?

SIZE UP A SPIRIT BY THE SWORD AND "THE" SPIRIT—I

John addresses his flock as "beloved" for the third of five times in this epistle (1 John 3:2, 21; 4:1, 7, 11). He confronts his sheep with a strict warning in 1 John 4:1: "do not believe every spirit, but test the spirits whether they are of God."

How do you size up a spirit? First, when you've heard a message spoken from a herald, you subsequently have to evaluate whether that communication derives from God or not. The apostle warns the saints at the end of 1 John 4:1 about the "many false prophets [who] have gone out in the world." Behind these purveyors of perdition who supposedly make proclamations in behalf of God is an underlying spirit.

John was gravely concerned, because of the vast numbers of these misrepresentatives of truth, that his much-loved saints might be deceived. Therefore he gave a standard whereby the truth could be discerned: "By this you know the Spirit of God: Every spirit that confesses that Jesus Christ has come in the flesh is of God" (1 John 4:2). The key question concerning someone's salvation or lack thereof consists of asking: Who is Jesus Christ? What an individual believes about Him reveals the spirit behind the message.

John's declaration "that Jesus Christ has come in the flesh" refutes the pre- form of Gnosticism taught in the first century; because the Gnostics believed all matter is evil, therefore God could not take on flesh. The words "has come" arise here in the perfect tense—a completed action in the past with the results continuing. Theologically, John taught that Jesus had taken on flesh (known as the incarnation), but that He remains in the glorified flesh as the God-Man. (More on this under relationship.)

The apostle's meaning in 1 John 4:1–2 was quite clear; he knew that the only way to evaluate the invisible spirit behind the messenger was to test the communication and discern if Jesus the Messiah left heaven to become a man. To deny this explicit teaching of the gospels and the remainder of the Bible on this key issue would unveil that the spirit didn't derive from God, and that the emissary of these lies should be classified as a false prophet.

What conclusion did John draw about those who denied the humanity of Jesus? He shared, "and every spirit that does not confess that Jesus Christ has come in the flesh is not of God. And this is the *spirit* of the Antichrist, which you have heard was coming, and is now already in the world" (1 John 4:3). After 2,000 years, the "spirit of the Antichrist" is alive and well and points to the coming Antichrist, who will renounce the deity of Jesus and proclaim himself god.

As we transition to 1 John 4:4–6 let me ask: Should we be afraid because of all the false prophets and the spirit of Antichrist that prevails today? Certainly not, John boldly reassures his flock: "You are of God, little children, and have overcome them, because He who is in you is greater than he who is in the world." The "you" is emphatic, to assure the saints that they were born again "and have overcome" the false prophets.

I like what the great missionary Hudson Taylor said about the nature of God's children. "We are a supernatural people, born again by a supernatural birth; we wage a supernatural fight and are taught by a supernatural teacher, led by a supernatural captain to assured victory." He understood the enabling power of God's indwelling Holy Spirit—just as John did, as he also assured the saints of triumph over the prince of darkness "because He [the Holy Spirit] who is in you is greater than he [Satan] who is in the world."

John emphatically points out, "They [the false prophets] are of the world." By using two emphatic statements in 1 John 4:4–5, he decisively shows that believers are of God, whereas the false prophets belong to this world's system, headed by Satan. That's why he added, "Therefore they speak as of the world, and the world hears them." Their message connects with the unsaved world that welcomes them with open arms.

The discerning apostle then uses a third emphatic remark in 1 John 4:6, "We are of God." "We" refers to the genuine teachers, namely the apostles, as does the following "us," in "He who knows God hears us." Again,

John, the master of stark contrasts, offers, "he who is not of God does not hear us." Simply stated, those who were Christians received John's message, and those who didn't belonged to the devil. His conclusion: "By this we know the spirit of truth and the spirit of error."

I hope that you jubilantly praise the Lord for God's indwelling lie-detecting device, the Holy Spirit, and are ready to study 1 John 4:1–6 in the broader context of Scriptural relationship.

SIZE UP A SPIRIT BY THE SWORD AND "THE" SPIRIT—R

John didn't want the saints at Ephesus to be gullible, so he wrote, "Beloved, do not believe every spirit, but test the spirits, whether they are of God; because many false prophets have gone out into the world" (1 John 4:1). Satan is a master manipulator who has dispatched a plethora of pseudo-prophets to deceive as many people as possible.

The apostle Paul likewise warned against the devil's ambassadors in 2 Corinthians 11:13–15: "For such are false apostles, deceitful workers, transforming themselves into apostles of Christ. And no wonder! For Satan himself transforms himself into an angel of light. Therefore *it is* no great thing if his ministers also transform themselves into ministers of righteousness, whose end will be according to their works." We need to heed both apostles, and to be on guard from those who proclaim a message contradictory to the gospel of Jesus Christ.

Earlier we studied that the spirit of Antichrist has been in operation for two millennia. In John's vicinity of ministry some were denying the humanity of Jesus; however, there were other doctrinally incorrect theologies being propagated broadly both then and now. Paul stated, "Now the Spirit expressly says that in the latter times some will depart from the faith, giving heed to deceiving spirits and doctrines of demons" (1 Tim. 4:1). Observe how Paul connects the dots between bad doctrine and fallen angels (demons).

You might be wondering, what other messages did the prince of darkness float around in the first century that still get disseminated today? Continuing in 1 Timothy 4, Paul gave two prevalent heresies associated with the Gnostic belief that matter was bad and spirit was good, "forbidding to marry, and *commanding* to abstain from foods which God created to be received with thanksgiving by those who believe and know the truth" (1 Tim. 4:3).

It should be noted that voluntary singleness and eating correctly have their advantages. The unattached person can give himself or herself fully to God's work without being distracted. Paul opined on this in 1 Corinthians 7:32–33, "He who is unmarried cares for the *things that belong* to the Lord—how he may please the Lord. But he who is married cares about the things of the world—how he may please his wife." Additionally, having a healthy manner of life through eating well and exercise can help the child of God to be a good custodian of the body entrusted to him, which houses the Holy Spirit.

Let's address dietary regulations first. We are no longer under the food laws of the Old Testament. Jesus came to fulfill the law, which frees us from such things as practicing animal sacrifices, and refraining from the strict eating prohibitions pronounced in Leviticus 11. Paul testified, "For every creature of God *is* good, and nothing is to be refused if it is received with thanksgiving; for it is sanctified by the word of God and prayer" (1 Tim. 4:4–5). Our Lord taught Peter, the apostle to the Jews, in Acts 10:15, "What God has cleansed you must not call common," pertaining to all foods specifically and the Gentiles by implication.

Moreover, today we have religious movements that endorse celibacy. God Himself contradicted this position in Genesis 2:18, "It is not good that man should be alone." Yet some would claim based upon their view of the Bible and tradition that to serve God in certain roles, that person must be single. Paul quickly disavowed that practice in 1 Timothy 4, showing that this teaching doesn't come from God but the evil one.

As John develops his thought about satanic deception in 1 John 4, he also writes how to test for a godly spirit behind the herald, "Every spirit that confesses that Jesus Christ has come in the flesh is of God" (verse 2). We observed earlier that "has come" carries the concept that Jesus had taken on flesh in the past, and remains in the flesh. John bolsters this doctrine in 2 John 7, "For many deceivers have gone out into the world who do not confess Jesus Christ *as* coming in the flesh." Here the apostle uses the present tense verb for "coming," showing that He still remains in the flesh.

How astonishing that God became man. The brilliant apostle Paul shared this truth and marveled at it in 1 Timothy 3:16, "And without controversy great is the mystery [a secret from the past that is now revealed] of godliness: God was manifested in the flesh, justified in the Spirit, seen by angels, preached among the Gentiles, believed on in the world, received up in glory." Our opening section in 1 John affirms the truth of Jesus' incarnation based upon the apostle's eyewitness testimony. In the Gospel of John the apostle of love shared, "And the Word became flesh and dwelt among us, and we beheld His glory, the glory as of the only begotten of the Father, full of grace and truth" (John 1:14).

On a personal note, I love thinking about Jesus as my mediator and High Priest—that He became like me so that eventually I could become like Him. He understands my human condition. "For we do not have a High Priest who cannot sympathize with our weaknesses, but was in all *points* tempted as *we are, yet* without sin" (Heb. 4:15). Also note how Paul describes Jesus in this role in 1 Timothy 2:5, "For *there is* one God and one Mediator between God and men, the Man Christ Jesus." Even at the right hand of the Father, our Lord is "the Man Christ Jesus." I remember preaching about this through an interpreter to a Hispanic congregation. My translator later shared with me that it was hard to keep translating once he had heard this truth, because it was so profound.

My beloved brother or sister, as we continue to carefully evaluate all the voices calling out to us, let's stop and pause over Jesus taking on flesh, and ponder the great truth that the God-Man ever lives to intercede for us, according to Hebrews 7:25. Great truths are not only to be mulled over, but also acted upon. So let's begin.

SIZE UP A SPIRIT BY THE SWORD AND "THE" SPIRIT—E

Spiritually mature saints evaluate all things by God's Word. Paul wrote, "But he who is spiritual judges all things, yet he himself is *rightly* judged by no one" (1 Cor. 2:15). John concurred with Paul's sentiment: "Beloved, do not believe every spirit, but test the spirits, whether they are of God; because many false prophets have gone out into the world" (1 John 4:1). Therefore, we need to carefully scrutinize the proclamations of all messengers who claim to speak for God, to discern the spirit behind the spokesperson.

Test all messages by God's Word, which derives from 1 John 4:1–3, gives us our first employment point. The most important aspect is to make sure someone correctly represents the gospel. For this reason I'm giving you 1 Corinthians 15:3–4, which is the most concise definition of the gospel in the New Testament, to memorize. It states, "For I delivered to you first of all that which I also received: that Christ died for our sins according to the Scriptures, and that He was buried, and that He rose again the third day according to the Scriptures."

When an individual purports that he or she is giving a message showing the way of salvation, compare the content with 1 Corinthians 15:3–4. There are some critical questions you must ask. Is the gospel compromised because it is incomplete? In other words, do all the components that Paul and the other gospel writers give appear in the message? Also—and this fits with our section on relationship concerning those who command individuals to abstain from marriage and certain foods—does the subject matter add to the gospel? When works emerge on the scene in conjunction with the gospel of grace, it is no longer grace; the messenger has received his text from a deceiving spirit.

One more thing: Be wary of those who depict the Christian life as a playground and not a battlefield. Suffering is an integral part of the believer's experience and should be expected. Preachers who claim that God wants us to be happy all the time, increase financially, and remain in good health often ignore how Jesus, Paul, and the New Testament disciples experienced just the opposite. *Test all messages by God's Word.*

Secondly, God has graciously implanted an internal mechanism to discern truth from lies; the Holy Spirit indwells each Christian and fulfills this role. *Triumph over false messengers by God's Spirit* becomes our second employment point, from 1 John 4:4–5. Staying close to God keeps us sensitive to His Spirit's guidance within and should not be discounted.

I remember decades ago when I was a new believer, hearing a man preach about the Christian being judged for his sins at the judgment seat of Christ. (Our works will be assessed, according to 1 Corinthians 3:11–15, because Jesus already paid the price for our sins!) In my youth I played a fair amount of pinball; this was (back in the day) when you could actually slightly shake the machine, for your advantage. If you jolted the machine too hard, the tilt message appeared and you lost the ability to use your paddles on that ball. May I say that when this man spoke, something inside said "tilt." The Lord loves to direct His children. Abide in Him and permit the Spirit to be your guide.

Here's our third employment point: *Trust God's Word to reveal truth and expose error*, which is based upon 1 John 4:6. Let's rehearse this helpful verse, "We are of God. He who knows God hears us; he who is not of God does not hear us. By this we know the spirit of truth and the spirit of error." Jesus had decades earlier told His apostles that it was imperative that He go away. He gave a reason for the necessity of His departure, "However, when He, the Spirit of truth has come, He will guide you into all truth" (John 16:13).

Never minimize the importance of illumination. This is the function of the Holy Spirit, who turns the light on concerning the Scripture that we may understand its meaning. Having this objective standard enables us to measure what people say by the Word of God, to know whether it consists of truth or error. As you daily spend time in the Bible, ask God to help you, via the Holy Spirit, to understand what you've read. Then trust Him to use this measuring stick in your life to avoid deception and error and to keep you walking in the truth.

CHAPTER FOURTEEN

RESPONDING CORRECTLY TO GOD'S LOVE

1 JOHN 4:7–12

———≈≈≈———

There was a professor of psychology who had no children of his own. Yet whenever he saw a neighbor scolding a child for some wrongdoing he would say, "You should love your child, not punish him." One hot summer afternoon the professor was doing some repair work on a concrete driveway leading to his garage. Tired out after several hours of work, he laid down the trowel, wiped the perspiration from his forehead, and started toward the house.

Just then he saw a mischievous little boy putting his foot in the fresh cement. He rushed over, grabbed him, and was about to spank him severely when a neighbor leaned from the window and said, "Watch it, professor! Don't you remember? You must love the child!" At this the professor yelled back furiously, "I do love him in the abstract but not in the concrete!"

Love can also be measured in the concrete because we have an objective standard in 1 John 4:7–12. John has already written about love on many occasions up to this point. We will see his tenth utilization of the verb for love and the sixth usage of the noun in 1 John 4:7. That's a whole lot of love. Let's again allow the Word to sink into our hearts with a slow and deliberate reading of 1 John 4:7–12:

> Beloved, let us love one another, for love is of God; and everyone who loves is born of God and knows God. He who does not love does not know God, for God is love. In this the love of God was manifested toward us, that God has sent His only begotten Son into the world, that we might live through Him. In this is love,

not that we loved God, but that He loved us and sent His Son *to be* the propitiation for our sins. Beloved, if God so loved us, we also ought to love one another.

No one has seen God at any time. If we love one another, God abides in us, and His love has been perfected in us (1 John 4:7–12).

Dear friends, let us love one another, for love comes from God. Everyone who loves has been born of God and knows God. Whoever does not love does not know God, because God is love. This is how God showed his love among us: He sent his one and only Son into the world that we might live through him. This is love: not that we loved God, but that he loved us and sent his Son as an atoning sacrifice for^c our sins. Dear friends, since God so loved us, we also ought to love one another. No one has ever seen God; but if we love one another, God lives in us and his love is made complete in us (1 John 4:7–12, NIV).

THREE CONCRETE REASONS TO LOVE ONE ANOTHER—F

- Is God's person divided, since John said, "God is light" (1 John 1:5) and "God is love" (1 John 4:8)? In other words, can we divide God into parts?
- What do the words "only begotten Son" mean in 1 John 4:9?
- How should we "love one another," according to the context of 1 John 4:11?
- What is the significance of John writing, "No one has seen God at any time" in 1 John 4:12?

THREE CONCRETE REASONS TO LOVE ONE ANOTHER—I

John addresses his congregation as "beloved" in 1 John 4:7 for the fourth of five times in 1 John. After John lavishes his affection toward the saints, he exhorts, "let us love one another." Christians are not to hate each other as the world despises the saved (1 John 3:13). The reason for this focused sacrificial love is then given, "for love is of God." The love that John wrote about isn't a natural love but a divinely given love.

The apostle continues in 1 John 4:7, "and everyone who loves is born of God and knows God." "Loves" originates from the Greek present participle, and its continual presence shows that an individual has been born of God. The perfect tense verb "born" testifies that an individual was saved in the past and remains in that condition. This same person "knows"—has a regular experiential knowledge—of the Father.

Contrary to the saved person who loves and knows God, "He who does not love does not know God, for God is love" (1 John 4:8). John uses the same two verbs ("love" and "knows") that appear in verse 7. The person who doesn't habitually love demonstrates that he isn't born again and hasn't experientially known God in the past (the meaning of the aorist "know"). Our apostle of contrasts shows the dissimilarity of the unsaved individual who doesn't know God, as modeled by his unloving nature, with the Father who is described by the perfection or attribute of "love."

Who God is—a loving God—is now described by what he did, "In this the love of God was manifested toward us, that God has sent His only begotten Son into the world, that we might live through Him" (1 John 4:9). The NIV translates it, "God showed his love among us," while the NKJV offers, "God was manifested toward us." Which should be the preferred translation, "among us" or "toward us"? I believe neither would be the best choice here. The Greek words are better translated *in us,* as the renowned Greek scholar A. T. Robertson believed, and this is also how it appears in the NASB. The apostle counts himself among those who believed on Jesus and internally (as represented by "in us") possessed the gift of eternal life.

"Unique" or "one of a kind" is the meaning of "only begotten," referring to Jesus. Since our Lord was sinless, this makes Him to be the one and only Son of God. John gave the purpose for the unique Son's manifestation, "that we might live through Him." Not only does our eternal life come from Jesus, but also the more abundant life here and now that He had promised.

God took the initiative to reach out to us as lost sinners: "In this is love, not that we loved God, but that He loved us and sent His Son to be the propitiation for our sins" (1 John 4:10). John uses the emphatic "we," showing that it wasn't us who first loved God. Then he used the strong contrast (adversative) "but" to demonstrate that the Father reached out to us by sending Jesus "to be the propitiation for our sins." The noun "propitiation" testifies of Jesus shedding His blood on our behalf to appease the wrath of God. Only the one-of-a-kind Savior could fulfill God's perfect standards to offer His life to placate the Father's holy anger.

John then lovingly appeals to the saints, "Beloved, if God so loved us, we also ought to love one another" (1 John 4:11). The word "if" is a first class condition assuming the statement to be true. The verse could be stated, "Since God so loved us, we also ought to love one another." Once again John chooses the emphatic "we" to strongly point out that "we" have an obligation to love the brethren by laying down our lives for them if necessary, just as the sinless Son of Man did for us.

Why did John write, "No one has seen God at any time" at the beginning of 1 John 4:12? Perhaps one reason is that since God cannot be seen, He desires to become visibly known via the indwelling Holy Spirit who lives within us—and who enables you and me to perform benevolent acts for His body, the church, that are externally witnessed. John closes out 1 John 4:12 with, "If [a third class condition, which shows a real possibility] we love one another, God abides in us, and His love has been perfected in us." As we sincerely care for each other, God's presence resides in us, and His love then matures us.

We have been introduced to many facets of God's love up to this point. With each revealed truth given to us comes the responsibility to act upon it diligently. My brothers and sisters, I'm proud of you for all that you've learned and have applied from our study. Yet it isn't time for your retirement from Christianity—in fact, it *never* is. So let's move ahead and employ what John uncovered for us, so that our invisible God might be observed through our obedience.

THREE CONCRETE REASONS TO LOVE ONE ANOTHER—R

Who is God? We come to understand the nature of the Father by studying His attributes or perfections. In 1 John 1:5, John wrote positively, "God is light" and then shared the same concept negatively, "and in Him is no darkness at all." Light depicts God as pure, righteous, and holy. John revealed another facet of God's nature when he shared, "for God is love" in 1 John 4:8. The word "love" appears anarthrous in the Greek—that is, without the article represented by the word "the"—showing that love is a quality of God.

Be careful not to divide the person of God by separating His attributes, such as His mercy, love, and grace. Theologically speaking, God is a simple being. The doctrine of divine simplicity instructs that God exists without parts. So when we study God as light and love, they are not qualities that make up His being. He is not composite, made up of parts. Therefore it is inappropriate to say that God *has* grace, mercy, or love; rather, He *is* grace, mercy, and love.

There are two particular emphases I would like to share with you because "God is love." First, *God has demonstrated His love for mankind.* Perhaps the best-known Bible verse in the world testifies to this truth, "For God so loved the world that He gave His only begotten Son, that whoever believes in Him should not perish but have everlasting life" (John 3:16). The great theologian Paul concurred, "But God demonstrates His own love toward us, in that while we were still sinners, Christ died for us" (Rom. 5:8).

The Bible explicitly teaches that Jesus is God. On account of this He also manifests the attribute of love. Paul testified about our position in Christ when He wrote in Galatians 2:20, "I have been crucified with Christ; it is no longer I who live, but Christ lives in me; and the *life* which I now live in the flesh I live by faith in the Son of God, who loved me and gave Himself for me." Both Father and Son demonstrated their love for mankind by their gift to us, Jesus Christ. Our response: "Thanks *be* to God for His indescribable gift!"

God has demonstrated His love for mankind, which is an awesome testimony to His divine essence. Therefore, the second concept that I'd like to share with you is: *We must demonstrate our love for God.* John repeatedly communicates this throughout 1 John. Let me impart five ways that we can demonstrate our love for God.

First, obedience testifies to our love for God. Jesus told His disciples,

"If you love Me, keep My commandments" (John 14:15). John broadens this idea in 1 John 5:3, "For this is the love of God, that we keep His commandments. And His commandments are not burdensome."

Secondly, dear child of God, *demonstrate your love for God by loving His Word.* It is reported that Charles Spurgeon said, "A Bible which is falling apart usually belongs to someone who isn't." Can you feel the passion of the psalmist, who said, "And I will delight myself in Your commandments, which I love" (Ps. 119:47)? Saturate yourself in God's Word and let it imbue your soul.

The third way we exemplify our love for God is to *love our neighbor.* The Old Testament law gave this command in Leviticus 19:18, "Love your neighbor as yourself." Jesus summed up the essence of the law with two commandments. The first was to love God with our entire being. "And the second, like *it*, is this: '*You shall love your neighbor like yourself*'" (Mark 12:31). When Jesus uses the word "like," it means "one and the same." That is, the second command is equal to the first, because loving our visible neighbor shows that we love the invisible God.

If we truly love God, we'll love our enemy as Jesus commanded becomes our fourth means to show our love for the Father. Consider these challenging words from the Master-Teacher, Jesus, in the Sermon on the Mount, "But I say to you, love your enemies, bless those who curse you, do good to those who hate you, and pray for those who spitefully use you and persecute you" (Matt. 5:44). Jesus did this; so must we.

The following and fifth manifestation of us loving God will sound familiar: *Love your Christian brothers and sisters.* Once again, enjoy the beauty of 1 John 4:7–9, "Beloved, let us love one another, for love is of God; and everyone who loves is born of God and knows God. He who does not love does not know God, for God is love. In this the love of God was manifested toward us, that God has sent His only begotten Son into the world, that we might live through Him." John's fellow apostle Peter would also give further revelation on this subject, "And above all things have fervent love for one another, for *love will cover a multitude of sins*" (1 Pet. 4:8).

You've just received some general ways to reveal your love for God. Let's get specific about the application of 1 John 4:7–12, concerning three concrete reasons to love one another.

THREE CONCRETE REASONS TO LOVE ONE ANOTHER—E

Employment point number one should stand out clearly because of what we've just studied under relationship. *Love one another because God is love* derives from 1 John 4:7–8.

In 1 Corinthians 13, Paul makes the argument that you can have all the gifting in the world, but if you lack love, then in essence, you have nothing. In particular, I want you to read 1 Corinthians 13 every day for one week, and petition God to saturate your mind with His love so that you can exhibit it to others.

Our second point of employment flows smoothly from the first: *Love one another because God sent Jesus* is based upon 1 John 4:9–11. What did it cost God to create the world? Actually, He spoke it into existence and He didn't suffer any loss personally. Now, what sacrifice *did* the Father provide for our salvation? "In this the love of God was manifested toward us, that God has sent His only begotten Son into the world, that we might live through Him" (1 John 4:9). The price that God paid for our redemption was costly; He gave that which was most precious to Him—Jesus Christ, the eternal Son of God.

God has always been a pursuer of the wayward, as the lover of our soul. When Adam sinned, God tracked down His insubordinate resident in the Garden of Eden that He might restore him spiritually. Similarly the Father initiated a way for us to be brought back to a right relationship with Him. We shouldn't ever forget that our loving Lord pursued us that He might redeem us. For this reason I want you to memorize 1 John 4:10: "In this is love, not that we loved God, but that He loved us, and sent His Son *to be* the propitiation for our sins."

I love the progression of thought in our passage. We began with loving God based upon who He is, and then moved forward to love Him on account of what He has done for us. Our third application, like the first two, is concrete. *Love one another because God dwells in us and perfects us* imparts to us employment point number three, from 1 John 4:11–12. All three applications aren't abstract concepts of God's love, but tangible means to display our love for God based upon who Jesus is, and what He's done for us.

Jesus came to reveal the Father. John 1:18 reports, "No one has seen God at any time. The only begotten Son, who is in the bosom of the Father, He has declared Him." If it weren't for the Son's incarnation, we would never have known the depth of God's character. Likewise John wrote in 1 John 4:12, "No one has seen God at any time." Since God's essence isn't visible to our physical sight, He allows the implanted Holy Spirit within us to mature us, with the results visibly revealing His nature.

Do you remember Jesus' discussion with Philip? "Philip said to Him, 'Lord, show us the Father, and it is sufficient for us.' Jesus said to him, 'Have I been with you so long, and yet you have not known Me, Philip? He who has seen Me has seen the Father'" (John 14:8–9). Right now, I'd like you to bow your head, and from the heart, talk to God. Thank Him for the Holy Spirit who lives within you. Tell Him that you desire His love to transform your life and make you mature, and that you want Him to openly display God's love through your yielded life. He will honor that sincere offer, my friend.

CHAPTER FIFTEEN

FREE SPEECH ON THE DAY OF JUDGMENT

1 JOHN 4:13–21

⟫⟫⟫⟫∼∼∼∼⟪⟪

A golfer's errant shot ended up on an anthill. He squared up, took a big swing—and missed. Thousands of innocent ants were killed. The novice golfer took another swing—and missed again. Another wave of ants was destroyed. Panic-stricken insects scurried everywhere.

One ant finally took charge. "Follow me," he cried with authority.

Another ant yelled, "But where are we going?"

He pointed to the golf ball sitting in front of them. "There. If we don't get on the ball, we're going to die!"

John has restated some of his popular themes of his epistle in our passage. Essentially he is saying, "It is time to get on the ball." Let's take the first step toward getting on the ball by reading 1 John 4:13–21:

> By this we know that we abide in Him, and He in us, because He has given us of His Spirit. And we have seen and testify that the Father has sent the Son *as* Savior of the world. Whoever confesses that Jesus is the Son of God, God abides in him, and he in God. And we have known and believed the love that God has for us. God is love, and he who abides in love abides in God, and God in him.
>
> Love has been perfected among us in this: that we may have boldness in the day of judgment; because as He is, so are we in this world. There is no fear in love; but perfect love casts out fear, because fear involves torment. But he who fears has not been made perfect in love. We love Him because He first loved us.

If someone says, "I love God," and hates his brother, he is a liar; for he who does not love his brother whom he has seen, how can he love God whom he has not seen? And this commandment we have from Him: that he who loves God *must* love his brother also (1 John 4:13–21).

By this we know that we abide in Him and He in us, because He has given us of His Spirit. We have seen and testify that the Father has sent the Son *to be* the Savior of the world.

Whoever confesses that Jesus is the Son of God, God abides in him, and he in God. We have come to know and have believed the love which God has for us. God is love, and the one who abides in love abides in God, and God abides in him. By this, love is perfected with us, so that we may have confidence in the day of judgment; because as He is, so also are we in this world. There is no fear in love; but perfect love casts out fear, because fear involves punishment, and the one who fears is not perfected in love. We love, because He first loved us. If someone says, "I love God," and hates his brother, he is a liar; for the one who does not love his brother whom he has seen, cannot love God whom he has not seen. And this commandment we have from Him, that the one who loves God should love his brother also (1 John 4:13–21, NASB).

THREE ASPECTS OF MUTUALLY EXPERIENCING GOD—F

- How has God "given us of His Spirit," according to 1 John 4:13?
- Did Jesus become the "Son of God" at His birth or is He eternally "the Son of God" (1 John 4:15)?
- What does John mean that "love has been perfected among us in this" from 1 John 4:17?
- What is the opposite of "love," from 1 John 4:18?
- Does John have someone (or a particular group) in mind when he writes, "If someone says, 'I love God'" and then practices hate, from 1 John 4:20?

Three Aspects of Mutually Experiencing God—I

A key word to explain what transpires in this passage is "mutual." It communicates something held in common by two or more parties. Amazingly, our text conveys, "By this we know that we abide in Him, and He in us, because He has given us of His Spirit" (1 John 4:13). The miraculous concept that "we know that we abide in Him, and He in us" boggles the mind.

To begin with, the Greek term translated "we know" is the verb we've seen often in John referring to experiential knowledge. There exists an objective way to understand "that we abide in Him, and He in us." John stated the source of this internal information, "Because He has given us of His Spirit." Moreover, the word "of," in speaking about "His Spirit," is called a partitive genitive by Greek grammarians and shows the whole, which is divided. God has taken the whole of the Holy Spirit and given us a share, much like a company that parcels out shares of stock to its employees.

John continues in 1 John 4:14, "And we have seen and testify that the Father has sent the Son *as* Savior of the world." The apostle uses the word "we" emphatically. Some believe "we" refers only to the apostles who literally saw Jesus, whom the Father dispatched to earth. Yet the references to "we" in 1 John 4:7–13 from our previous paragraph points to the community of believers, including John. Moreover, since God has "given us of His Spirit," as mentioned in the previous verse, all believers—not just the apostles—can "testify that the Father has sent the Son *as* Savior of the world."

Therefore, although no one has seen God in all His glory (1 John 4:12), the Christian has with his or her eyes of faith "seen" and "testify" (the present tense verbs show a continual witness) "that the Father has sent the Son *as* Savior of the world."

John gave another evidence of the mutual abiding, "Whoever confesses that Jesus is the Son of God, God abides in him, and he in God" (1 John 4:15). The individual who confesses, "Jesus is the Son of God," enjoys the Father's presence within, and also residing in Him. When the apostle wrote this epistle, Jesus had already ascended to the Father. Yet John used the present tense "is" concerning one's confession of Jesus currently being the Son of God—even when He returned to heaven. For this reason "is" implies that Jesus is the eternal Son. In other words, Jesus was eternally God's Son; He didn't become "the Son of God" at the incarnation but has always been, and will forever continue to be so.

The expression "Son of God" is a Hebraism—that is, a structure connected to the Hebrew language. "Son" belongs to the category "of God." Therefore the person who verbally expresses that Jesus is the Son of God because of an inner conviction is acknowledging that Jesus is God, and experiences the mutual abiding cited throughout our passage.

John begins 1 John 4:16 with another emphatic "we": "And we have known and believed the love that God has for us." The Greek words for "have known" and "believed" are both perfects—having known and believed in the past with that knowledge and faith continuing. Both the NKJV and NIV translate that God's love is "for us." The Greek preposition would better be translated as "in." This passage isn't showing God's love "for us" in sending Jesus to die on the cross, but the personal experience of His love "in us" by the indwelling Holy Spirit.

John finishes 1 John 4:16 with, "God is love, and he who abides in love abides in God, and God in Him." When we have a love-filled existence, we have a God-filled life. This section of John is replete with the concept of mutual abiding.

Continuing the theme of love, John writes, "Love has been perfected among us in this: that we may have boldness in the day of judgment" (1 John 4:17). We had learned earlier that "boldness" means all speech, and conveys a freedom of speech. At the rapture, God's abiding children, whose love has matured, can be ready to converse openly with Jesus and not be ashamed, because of their regular and intimate communion with Him.

John then shares a profound statement with many implications in the second half of 1 John 4:17: "Because as He is, so are we in this world." Our position in Jesus causes us to dwell with Him in the heavenly places, which gives the basis for experiencing this boldness. Jesus is the Son of God (verse 15), and we are God's children, too. That places us in our heavenly standing. Finally, as Jesus abided in the Father and experienced total victory, so can we through Him.

Since we have this confidence to stand before Jesus grounded upon our position, John adds, "There is no fear in love; but perfect love casts out fear, because fear involves torment. But he who fears has not been made perfect in love" (1 John 4:18). The opposite of love in our context is fear. When love vacates the premises, fear fills the vacuum, and brings torment into our lives. When a child of God is consumed with fear, it testifies to an immature or weakened love.

How can saints bolster their boldness? I'm glad you asked. "We love Him because He first loved us" (1 John 4:19). Once again, the "we" is emphatic. Dear brother or sister, deliberately ponder God's love for you; contemplate how He initiated it and why, and watch your fears drift away.

John is most likely taking a jab at the false prophets in 1 John 4:20: "If someone says, 'I love God,' and hates his brother, he is a liar; for he who does not love his brother whom he has seen, how can he love God whom he has not seen"? As we studied back in 1 John 3:16–17, when we close our compassion toward a needy brother or sister, our lives shout loudly that we don't know God. A sincere care for those saints lacking basic needs, like food and shelter, gives a glowing endorsement that we love the God who can't be seen with the naked eye.

John closes out our passage with a call to action, "And this commandment we have from Him: that he who loves God *must* love his brother also" (1 John 4:21). My dear extended family member, don't ever forget that to love God is to love your brother, and to love your brother is to love God; both are commanded through John. I trust you are ready to be stretched in your thinking as we broaden the scope of 1 John 4:13–21 in relationship to the rest of Scripture.

THREE ASPECTS OF MUTUALLY EXPERIENCING GOD—R

Since we've already spent much time looking at God's love toward us and our responsibility to the family of God, I thought we'd spend a bit more time examining the implications of 1 John 4:18. That text says, "There is no fear in love; but perfect love casts out fear, because fear involves torment. But he who fears has not been made perfect in love."

Can you remember a time when fear suddenly seized you? For me, the year was 1983. My wife Kim and I were on our honeymoon in Bermuda. (That wasn't the scary part!) It was late May and we wanted to enjoy some of the beautiful scenery, so we paid to have a glass-bottom-boat ride. It was exhilarating to be able to see fish swimming under our boat, as the clean water permitted us to watch the underwater activity.

After being in the boat for a while, the tour guide announced, "You are now in the Bermuda Triangle." (Another designation for this delightful tidbit of information is the Devil's Triangle.) Over the years, both planes and boats mysteriously have disappeared in this region. Since we were in a boat, the thought did cross my mind that now would be a good time to panic.

There exists a healthy fear; it is called the fear of the Lord. "The fear of the LORD is clean," reported the psalmist in Psalm 19:9, "enduring forever." However, there is an unhealthy fear that arises in one's heart because of a scarcity of God's love. Adam was the first person to use the word "afraid" in the Bible. After he disobeyed God, the Holy One said to him in Genesis 3:9, "Where are you?" (God doesn't ask a question because He doesn't know the answer, but because He is looking for a certain response.) Adam replied, "I heard Your voice in the garden, and I was afraid because I was naked, and I hid myself" (Gen. 3:10).

Adam's fear resulted from his disobedience to God. His lack of love for God, demonstrated by eating the forbidden fruit, not only impacted all of earth's inhabitants with a sin nature that is passed down from generation to generation, but also the inclination to fear because of the insecurity that emerges when God's love is rejected or ignored. Since the image of God was marred in man because of the fall, the process to restore the likeness begins when we place our faith in Christ. We then have a new capacity to have victory over the doubts that come our way from the wicked one, and from the nature of life itself.

Paul counseled the saints in Ephesians 4:22–24, "that you put off, concerning your former conduct, the old man which grows corrupt according to the deceitful lusts, and be renewed in the spirit of your mind, and that you put on the new man which was created according to God, in righteousness and true holiness." The renewing of the mind consists of being filled with the love of God. This is essential to overcoming fear. Fear is so prevalent in this life that the most repeated command in the Bible is "do not fear."

Even ministers of Jesus Christ experience fear. Paul told his son in the faith, Timothy, "For God has not given us a spirit of fear, but of power and of love and of a sound mind" (2 Tim. 1:7).

John also connects fear with "torment" in 1 John 4:18. Matthew 25:46 uses the same Greek word. Jesus spoke about the future judgment of the sheep and the goats; the goats—people who don't know Christ—will go "away into everlasting punishment." A more nuanced meaning of "torment" is "punishment."

Now that you are aware of the penalty for not allowing God's love to mature you, the employment points from 1 John 4:13–21 will instruct you how to overcome fear.

THREE ASPECTS OF MUTUALLY EXPERIENCING GOD—E

One of the joys of twenty-five years of pastoral ministry is mining the ore from the Word of God. There exists no other book in the universe—let alone one that's more than 2,000 years old—that is as relevant today as the day it was written.

With that in mind, let's begin with employment point number one: *Experience God mutually by His Spirit* is gleaned from 1 John 4:13–16. The idea of experiencing *God* derives from 1 John 4:13, "By this we know that we abide in Him, and He is us, because He has given us of His Spirit." That same verb appears in Matthew 1:25, describing Joseph and Mary knowing one another intimately after the birth of Jesus.

Through God's Holy Spirit, we are assured not only that we know that God abides in us but that we abide in Him. The Holy Spirit first indwells us at salvation. Subsequently He leads us (Rom. 8:14), bears fruit in us (Gal. 5:22–23), and fills us for joyful and victorious living (Eph. 5:18–19). Determine to abide in Christ, and He will do the same for you, and He will confirm this internally by the Spirit's presence.

Abiding is the key to spiritual growth and the expulsion of fear.

Employment point number two, from 1 John 4:17–18, is as follows: *Experience God mutually to expel fear.* In the preceding paragraph I mentioned that God's Spirit bears fruit in us. The first fruit mentioned in Galatians 5:22 is love, which when cultivated in your heart will drive out fear.

I'd like you to memorize four verses over the course of a month, two from the Old Testament and two from the New Testament. It generally takes a month to form a habit. On account of this I want you to memorize and meditate upon one verse each week. Here's memory verse number one, "Fear not, for I am with you; be not dismayed, for I am your God. I will strengthen you, yes, I will help you, I will uphold you with My righteous right hand" (Isa. 43:10).

Your second text also comes from Isaiah 43. It states, "For I, the LORD your God, will hold your right hand, saying to you, 'Fear not, I will help you'" (Isa. 43:10).

Now, moving on to your New Testament prescribed verses, here is your third memory verse: "For God has not given us a spirit of fear, but of power and of love and of a sound mind" (2 Tim. 1:7).

Finally from 1 John 4:18: "There is no fear in love; but perfect love casts out fear, because fear involves torment. But he who fears has not been made perfect in love." Walk with God and He will reside with you, and will fill you with love so that you can experience the liberation from fear.

Experience God mutually to love the brethren is our third employment point, from 1 John 4:19–21. Remember, "We love Him because He first loved us" (1 John 4:19). As a result of God's love touching the very nooks and crannies of your soul, you will be able to minister sincerely to your brothers and sisters in Christ with an unfeigned love.

John wrote, "And this commandment we have from Him: that he who loves God *must* love his brother also." Do you know a Christian brother or sister who has an immediate need? If so, right now, write down that person's name, and ask God to guide you to meeting that need. If you don't have the economic means to do so, then pray that God will provide what's needed. The longer you abide in God and He in you, the greater He will increase your love for the brethren. My special friend, let's get on the ball.

CHAPTER SIXTEEN
JOYFUL OBEDIENCE
1 JOHN 5:1–3

What's the image that comes to your mind when you think of a pastor? Perhaps the furthest thought from your mind is that of an athlete. I'm not sure what athletic ability the apostle Paul had, but he regularly used sporting illustrations in his writings. Paul captured the concept that discipline is necessary for any successful athlete and can build a wonderful bridge to ministry because it also requires a strict training regiment to accomplish that vocation.

The physical rigors I experienced to be modestly competent in the three sports that I've competed in have been used by the Lord to prepare me for a different set of disciplines, which would be necessary for the ministry. I loved baseball as a child and hoped to wind up in Cooperstown, New York to be inducted into the Baseball Hall of Fame. My local park, which housed six baseball fields, was only about 300 yards from my house. When I didn't have a game to play on the weekends, I would go to the sports complex and field balls for any group doing batting practice, which usually led them to pitch me some balls. I was fully committed to be a great baseball player and actually made it into Cooperstown, albeit at a much lower level. It was my privilege to be elected to the Babe Ruth League Hall of Fame and have my name put in a book housed in Cooperstown, with a plethora of other players, for my achievements. Some years later, it was fun taking my three boys there and having an employee to locate the book with my official statistics and family history to show them.

This young athlete also had another passion: tennis. During the summer months I would play six to eight hours each day. Because both sports are primarily played during the summer, when I had to choose between baseball and tennis I chose the latter. Now I had a new goal: to become a professional tennis player. I didn't make it but I ranked number one in my high school for my junior and senior years. Furthermore, I was ranked in the top eight countywide during my junior year in high school and was awarded the outstanding athlete of the year in tennis. The following year, when I became a senior, I ranked in the top four in the county. This was a long way from playing at Wimbledon, but for a young man who was self-taught and never had money to pay for lessons, it served (pun intended) to form much-needed patterns of discipline.

Growing up in a middle-class family presented a challenge to my tennis career because of limited funding. I couldn't afford to play indoor tennis during the winter months; therefore, I took up weightlifting and jogging at the local YMCA to train. To my knowledge, I was the only tennis player in the county during my junior and senior years that could easily bench-press more than 300 pounds. After high school I continued my weight lifting and several years later placed second in a bench-press competition. Eventually I could bench-press twice my weight, lifting 360 pounds while weighing 180 pounds. (By the way, did I mention that there were only two of us competing when I placed second in my bench-press competition?)

Why have I taken you through my three-sport ancient history? Because there exists a parallel between sporting competition and the testing that occurs throughout our Christian lives. If you train hard athletically, people will see your skill set when you're the contestant, and rewards generally follow. Likewise, if you are truly saved, there will be evidence that you are attached to Jesus, even during the trials of life.

A triathlon is a singular competition with three separate events. John addressed salvation as a singular entity with three different aspects in 1 John 5:1–3. Let's take a closer look:

> Whoever believes that Jesus is the Christ is born of God, and whoever loves the Father loves the *child* born of Him. By this we know that we love the children of God, when we love God and observe His commandments. For this is the love of God, that we keep His commandments; and His commandments are not burdensome (1 John 5:1–3).

Everyone who believes that Jesus is the Christ has been fathered by God, and everyone who loves the father loves the child fathered by him. By this we know that we love the children of God: whenever we love God and obey his commandments. For this is the love of God: that we keep his commandments. And his commandments do not weigh us down (1 John 5:1–3, NET)

THE CHRISTIAN TRIATHLON—F

- "Him" is used three times at the end of 1 John 5:1. Who is the referent in each case?
- What do the words "By this" point to in 1 John 5:2?
- What is the meaning of the word "burdensome" in 1 John 5:3?

THE CHRISTIAN TRIATHLON—I

The adjective "whoever" in "Whoever believes that Jesus is the Christ is born of God" (1 John 5:1) refers to every individual. In his gospel, John often used the present tense participle "believes" as the prerequisite for salvation. Yet that isn't the emphasis here.

Let me share my Greek translation of 1 John 5:1a: "Whoever is believing that Jesus is the Messiah, has been born of God." In other words, when a person has been fathered by God—spiritually been born again—that individual continues to believe that Jesus is the Christ. The NET is correct in translating the perfect passive participle as "has been," whereas the NKJV incorrectly gives "is," which would mean the verb is present tense. Simply stated, to continually believe in Jesus as the Messiah results from being born again.

Born-again believers know "that Jesus is the Christ." The name "Jesus" refers to the historical person and, "is the Christ" testifies that even now He is God's anointed one. John continued, "and everyone who loves Him who begot also loves him who is begotten of Him" (1 John 5:1b). The love spoken about moves the believer to gaze both in a vertical and horizontal direction. First, consider the vertical relationship; "everyone who loves Him" directs us upward to love God the Father. Second, consider the horizontal connection that when a believer loves the Father that he "also loves him [a fellow Christian] who is begotten of Him" [the Father].

First John 4:2 states, "By this we know that we love the children of God, when we love God and keep His commandments." "By this" or "in this" now appears for the sixth and final time in 1 John (1 John 2:3; 3:10, 16, 19; 4:17; 5:2). Four of the six occurrences are used with the verb "know" (1 John 2:3; 3:16, 19; 5:2), which again infers experiential knowledge. John gives two measurable means to know experientially that we love God's children: by loving God, and by practicing His commandments.

The Greek word that appears both for loving God's children and for loving the Father is the same one. Both times it occurs in the exact same form in the present tense. This isn't the verb that speaks of a friendship kind of love, but *love with the focus of the will carrying a strong affection*. John demonstrated that to love the Father means to love His children, and that the two are inseparable.

At the same time, the objective standard for understanding that you love God's children is when you "keep His commandments." The present tense verb "keep" shows a continual guarding of His mandates, as a warden does over his prisoners. To summarize 1 John 4:2: Exemplify your love for the saints by habitually loving God and by keeping His commandments.

John seems to be carrying this thought over into 1 John 5:3: "For this is the love of [for] God, that we keep His commandments. And His commandments are not burdensome." John uses the objective genitive (love for God) and not the subjective genitive (love from God). And once again, John uses the verb "keep" as he did in 1 John 5:2. Not only are God's commandments to be observed, but they shouldn't be "burdensome." The usage here conveys that God's commandments shouldn't be viewed as a cumbersome obligation. We will further build upon John's teaching in our next section on relationship.

THE CHRISTIAN TRIATHLON—R

I remember hearing the story many years ago about a translator who was working in a foreign land with the aim of translating the Bible into the local dialect. This faithful worker for the Lord grew in frustration because he couldn't find an equivalent for the word "obedience." Heading home one day, discouraged because of his unsuccessful attempts to find a match for that term, he reached his property line, where his dog greeted him with wagging tail. The master threw a stick for the dog to fetch that he retrieved quickly. When a local man saw this, he said, "Your dog is all ears." The translator now had his word for obedience.

John desired all his children to obey God's Word unconditionally. He wrote, "For this is the love of God, that we keep His commandments. And His commandments are not burdensome." Our beloved apostle, who had reclined on Jesus' bosom at the Last Supper, had learned well from his beloved Master. In John's old age, he experienced banishment to the Isle of Patmos, where he'd receive the book of Revelation. Seven times to the same number of churches, Jesus commanded, "He who has an ear, let him hear what the Spirit says to the churches" (Rev. 2:7, 11, 17, 29; 3:6, 13, 22). As the man had a dog that was all ears, Jesus required His followers to "have an ear" and to obey.

As mentioned earlier, the word "keep" means "to watch over," in the sense of a warden. Focus your attention how the verb appears twice in Acts 12:5-6. "Peter was therefore kept in prison, but constant prayer was offered to God for him by the church. And when Herod was about to bring him out, that night Peter was sleeping, bound with two chains between two soldiers; and the guards before the door were keeping the prison." In the same way that Peter was carefully guarded in prison, we should likewise keep God's commandments with the same vigilance.

Upon hearing that we should obey the Lord's commandments, the directive could seem generic and non-personal. Paul helped on this front by giving a summation of the commandments in Romans 13:9, which shows the specificity of the Bible, "For the commandments, 'You shall not commit adultery.' 'You shall not murder.' 'You shall not steal.' 'You shall not bear false witness,' 'You shall not covet,' and if *there is* any other commandment, are *all* summed up in this saying, namely, 'You shall love your neighbor as yourself.'" Now that the commandments have been summed up, let's consider our attitude toward them.

John adds, "And His commandments are not burdensome" (1 John 5:3). Do you find that obeying the Scripture is a delight, or like carrying heavy furniture up ten flights of steps? The Old Testament high priests had an annual responsibility on the Day of Atonement to offer a sacrifice for their personal sin, and then another one for all of Israel. It technically didn't cost them anything to comply with the precepts from the book of Leviticus. Not so with our great High Priest, Jesus Christ.

The psalmists prophesied about Jesus' sacrifice for our sin, and the mindset that He would portray in bearing our transgressions. Psalm 40:6–8 reveals, "Sacrifice and offering You did not desire; my ears You have opened; burnt offering and sin offering You did not require. Then I said, 'Behold, I come; in the scroll of the Book it is written of me. I delight to do Your will, O my God, and your law is within my heart.'" Jesus found it a "delight," and not a "burden" to obey the will of His Father. Let's display such a godly attitude when it comes to keeping the Lord's commandments.

I'm confident that you know what is coming, since we've made this long but I hope most prosperous journey through 1 John together. We shouldn't be content with just knowing God's Word; we must now take what we've learned and joyfully put it into practice.

THE CHRISTIAN TRIATHLON—E

How do we, as born-again Christians, model that we belong to Jesus? The answer is simply by showcasing our Christian virtues throughout our lives. Like an athlete competing in a triathlon—one competition with three events—we have a singular challenge, living a faithful Christian existence, with three virtuous practices: faith, love, and obedience.

Demonstrate your salvation through faith, from 1 John 5:1, becomes our first employment point. Again, because of the accuracy of the translation, let's look at 1 John 5:1 in the NET version, "Everyone who believes that Jesus is the Christ has been fathered by God." The Greek text conveys that since God's children have been born again (in the past) that they will continue (in the present) to believe that Jesus is the Messiah. So one way to make known that you are truly saved consists of exemplifying faith in your daily life.

First, I want you to memorize the definition of faith that I've used for decades: *taking God at His Word and acting upon it.* God honors those who embrace His promises by believing them. When God told Abram (later Abraham) that his seed would become as numerous as the stars of heaven, Genesis 15:6 reports, "he believed in the LORD, and He accounted it to him for righteousness." God the Father deposited righteousness into Abraham's account as a result of the father of faith *taking God at His Word and acting upon it.* Your assignment is to apply the definition of faith to God's promises, because his Word is his bond.

The church of Jesus Christ has a vast amount of promises from God. Peter wrote, "by which have been given us exceedingly great and precious promises" (2 Pet. 1:4). Claim them daily, my friends, and the Lord will be pleased with your life. Remember Hebrews 11:6, "But without faith *it is* impossible to please *Him,* for he who comes to God must believe that He is, and *that* He is a rewarder of those who diligently seek Him."

A daily faith in the living God, leaning upon His promises, shows your salvation. The second employment point does the same: *Demonstrate your salvation through love* (1 John 5:2). This second application easily flows from John's pen to our lives, "By this we know that we love the children of God, when we love God and keep His commandments." Faith has great value in this life; love is more expansive, having incomprehensible worth both now and throughout eternity.

Paul gives a series of overstatements (hyperbole) in 1 Corinthians 13:1–3 to show the superiority of love, which is eternal, to spiritual gifts, which are temporal. Let's examine 1 Corinthians 13:1–2: "Though I speak with the tongues of men and of angels, but have not love, I have become as sounding brass or a clanging cymbal. And though I have the *gift* of prophecy, and understand all mysteries and all knowledge, and though I have all faith, so that I could remove mountains, but have not love, I am nothing." No one has the abilities Paul just cited; he uses hyperbole to show the vital importance of deeming love even more important than spiritual gifts that won't be necessary in heaven. He closes out the chapter with, "And now abide faith, hope, love, these three, but the greatest of these is love" (1 Cor. 13:13). Why does love rate so highly? Because "Love never fails," according to the apostle in 1 Corinthians 13:8—because it is eternal in nature.

Your second mission, therefore, is to learn 1 Corinthians 13:13 by heart. Why? If the appropriate use of spiritual gifts is vital to a healthy church, how much more vital is our love for God and man, which has eternal ramifications? Allow the glorious words of 1 Corinthians 13:13 to permeate your thinking, and permit the Spirit of God to motivate you to *demonstrate your salvation through love.*

Have you become all ears? That is: How committed are you to obeying God's Word in its entirety? *Demonstrate your salvation through obedience* is our third and final employment point, which derives from 1 John 5:3. I've given you some memory work in this chapter—why not retain one more great verse? Let's also deposit 1 John 5:3 in our storage bank for future recall: "For this is the love of God, that we keep His commandments. And His commandments are not burdensome."

My beloved brother or sister, our salvation is a gift that keeps on giving. As a result of what has been entrusted to us, like a good athlete who displays his abilities during a sporting event, we should model the glorious triad of faith, love, and obedience that testifies to our new nature in Christ.

CHAPTER SEVENTEEN

VICTORY IN CHRIST

1 JOHN 5:4–5

=⌇∿⌇=

A horse-racing fan was telling his pal about his latest day at the track. "I went out to the track and it was the eleventh day of the eleventh month. I got there exactly at 11:00 a.m. My daughter was eleven years old that day and the eleventh race had eleven horses. I put all the money I had on the eleventh horse on the card."

His friend asked, "And that horse won?"

"No," the racing fan replied. "He came in eleventh."

Victory is never guaranteed to the gambler. Yet being a world-conqueror is assured to the child of God. In our last chapter we learned about three aspects of being born again. We will now observe how the saints experience sustained victory over this world's system through Jesus in 1 John 5:4–5.

> For whatever is born of God overcomes the world. And this is the victory that has overcome the world—our faith. Who is he who overcomes the world, but he who believes that Jesus is the Son of God? (1 John 5:4–5).

> Every child of God can defeat the world, and our faith is what gives us this victory. No one can defeat the world without having faith in Jesus as the Son of God (1 John 5:4–5, CEV).

HOW TO BE A WORLD-CONQUEROR—F

- Why did John write, "Whatever is born of God overcomes the world" and not "Whoever is born of God overcomes the world" in 1 John 5:4?

- What specifically does the term "overcome" mean in "overcomes the world" in 1 John 5:4?
- Why does John then say, "Who is he who overcomes the world" in 1 John 5:5, when he asked in 1 John 5:4, "Whatever is born of God overcomes the world?"
- What exactly does it mean that Jesus "is the Son of God" in 1 John 5:5?

HOW TO BE A WORLD-CONQUEROR—I

Why did John use the neuter "whatever" instead of the expected masculine "whoever" when he wrote, "For whatever is born of God overcomes the world" in 1 John 5:4? The apostle most likely used the neuter to emphasize the quality of being "born of God" instead of pointing to the victorious individual himself triumphing over this world's system. On account of this John showed that the new nature implanted by the Holy Spirit fosters the enablement for the saint to not submit to the allurements of the world. The present tense for "overcomes" testifies that all true believers in Jesus Christ can consistently prevail over the world.

The instrument that God uses for our regular success over the current age is cited in 1 John 5:4b: "And this is the victory that has overcome the world—our faith." Whereas John uses the present tense verb "overcomes" in the first part of the verse modeling our habitual winning over Satan's inducements, he uses the same verb but in the aorist form, representing an overcoming that started in the past. That is, the aorist points back to the believer's salvation; at that moment he or she became an overcomer. Your faith in Christ qualifies you to be a world-conqueror.

John then asks and answers his own question in 1 John 5:5: "Who is he who overcomes the world, but He who believes that Jesus is the Son of God? Again, John turns toward faith as the means to achieve victory. Specifically and pointedly, the apostle directs the overcomer to believe that the historical Jesus is currently also the Son of God. The present tense verb "is" declares that Jesus remains the "Son of God" even now. First John 5:1 had drawn our attention to Jesus being God's anointed one as the Christ (Messiah); in 1 John 5:5, the apostle zeros in on the deity of Jesus by calling Him "the Son of God."

Under relationship we'll probe our victory in Christ as a world-conqueror, through our salvation in the Son of God.

How to Be a World-Conqueror—R

Are all Christians overcomers, according to the teaching of the New Testament? John answers with a resounding yes: "For whatever is born of God overcomes the world" (1 John 5:4). The new birth relegates the child of God to the classification of victor. Jesus spoke about two births—the physical and then the spiritual—in John 3 while dialoging with Nicodemus. He declares in John 3:6-7, "That which is born of the flesh is flesh, and that which is born of the Spirit is spirit. Do not marvel that I said to you [the singular "you" refers to Nicodemus], you [the plural "you" addresses all people] must be born again." The indwelling Holy Spirit resides within each believer and assures the saint that God will complete what He's begun.

The word "overcomes" emerges twenty-eight times in the New Testament. Each of the seven churches in Asia Minor at the beginning of the book of Revelation was given a promise or promises as recipients of the gift of eternal life. The directed pledge to an individual church pertained to all churches because to all seven the words of Jesus were given, "He who has an ear, let him hear what the Spirit says to the churches" (Rev. 2:7, 11, 17, 29; 3:6, 13, 22). We'll briefly consider what God has in store for us in the future.

Jesus said in Revelation 2:7 to the church of Ephesus, "To him who overcomes I will give to eat from the tree of life, which is in the midst of the Paradise of God." Since the tree of life will be in the New Jerusalem (Rev. 22:2), we will partake of its joys in that supernal city. Then to the church of Smyrna Jesus offered, "He who overcomes shall not be hurt by the second death" (Rev. 2:11). The words "shall not" in the Greek derive from what is called emphatic negation. It is the strongest way to say that believers won't experience the Lake of Fire. The first death refers to physical death and the second to eternal separation from God. We are eternally secure in Jesus.

We find Jesus' third promise given to the church of Pergamos in Revelation 2:17: "To him who overcomes I will give some of the hidden manna to eat. And I will give him a white stone, and on the stone a new name written which no one knows except him who receives it." God provided manna for the nation of Israel's sustenance in Exodus 16. We will enjoy special heavenly provision in the New Jerusalem. Moreover, there are some surprises awaiting us that speak about our future intimacy with the Lord in our coming dwelling place. One of the things I love about the book of Revelation is that God has some special treats for us upon arriving home.

Next we have Jesus' fourth promise given to the church of Thyatira in Revelation 2:26–28: "And he who overcomes, and keeps My works until the end, to him I will give power over the nations—He shall rule them with a rod of iron; As the potter's vessels shall be broken to pieces—as I also have received from My Father; and I will give him the morning star." We've studied the rapture, when Jesus returns for the church, which will be followed by the tribulation. At the end of the seven-year period, Jesus will return with us to establish His kingdom on earth (Rev. 20). My dear brother and sister, we will rule and reign with Him.

The excitement builds as we study the fifth promise from Jesus to the church of Sardis in Revelation 3:5: "He who overcomes shall be clothed in white garments, and I will not blot out his name from the Book of Life; but I will confess his name before My Father and before His angels." Perhaps the white garments represent the perpetual state of purity that we'll enjoy throughout eternity. Also, the Son will testify to the Father that we belong to Him, again showing our secure position forever.

Some might have fear that we won't stay housed in the New Jerusalem endlessly. The sixth promise from Jesus to the church of Philadelphia again stresses our eternal security: "He who overcomes, I will make him a pillar in the temple of My God, and he shall go out no more. And I will write on him the name of My God and the name of the city of My God, the New Jerusalem, which comes down out of heaven from My God. And I will write on him My new name" (Rev. 3:12). The "pillar" shows permanence; and having Jesus write His Father's name on us indicates that we belong to Him everlastingly.

The seventh promise is shared with the church of Laodicea in Revelation 3:21: "To him who overcomes I will grant to sit with Me on My throne, as I also overcame and sat down with My Father on His throne." The Old Testament saints, and the saints who made that transition to the New Testament era, awaited God's future kingdom. We, and they, will enjoy Christ's millennial reign (Rev. 20) as well as the following creation of a new heaven and earth (Rev. 21–22).

I know that I have barely scratched the surface on Jesus' promises, but know that as overcomers we should do everything possible to faithfully walk with Him and serve Him now, in preparation for what is to come.

The aforementioned rewards are possible because of what's stated in 1 John 5:5: "Who is he who overcomes the world, but he who believes that Jesus is the Son of God?" The expression "Son of God" strongly declares that Jesus is God and that is why He can offer us this future hope. Let's anticipate our bright future because of our relationship with God's eternal Son, who is "the same, yesterday, today, and forever."

Ready to shift gears and move toward our employment? Here we go....

How to Be a World-Conqueror—E

Believer, overcome the world through faith is our first employment point, from 1 John 5:4. Jesus made this statement, "These things I have spoken to you, that in Me you may have peace. In the world you will have tribulation; but be of good cheer, I have overcome the world" (John 16:33). Since Jesus triumphed over this world, we don't fight *for* victory but *from* victory. Even death can't extinguish the new life Christ has given to us. In the context of resurrection, Paul wrote, "But thanks *be* to God, who gives us the victory through our Lord Jesus Christ" (1 Cor. 15:57).

Since we are continuing on the theme of faith, I want you to sequentially take each of the promises from Revelation 2–3, one a day, for the next seven days. Think about them throughout the day, and make sure that you meditate upon all seven of them in one week. Getting the big picture by faith will encourage you to be consistent in your Christian walk, knowing that no sacrifice is too large for the benefits that are before you.

The second employment point builds upon the first: *Believer, overcome the world through faith in God's Son* is taken from 1 John 5:5, where Jesus is called "the Son of God." Let me elaborate upon this term by what Jesus said in John 5:17, "My Father has been working until now, and I have been working." The hostile audience to whom He spoke understood that He claimed equality with God because Jesus called Him "My Father." Their response is given in John 5:18: "Therefore the Jews sought all the more to kill Him, because He not only broke the Sabbath [by healing on that day, according to their misinterpretation of the Old Testament], but also said that God was His Father, making Himself equal with God."

My dear friends, the Christian life can be challenging. You need to understand via faith that you must remain committed to this journey. Because of Paul's faith in Jesus and His promises, he could write in 1 Corinthians 15:58: "Therefore my beloved brethren, be steadfast, immovable, always abounding in the work of the Lord, knowing that your labor is not in vain in the Lord." By faith in the Son of God, tell Him that you will stay true to the Christian course right now, and daily apply 1 Corinthians 15:58. And then, watch what happens.

CHAPTER EIGHTEEN

ETERNALLY SECURE IN CHRIST
1 JOHN 5:6–13

⸺⸺

One day there was a man who was talking to God. The man wanted to know what eternity is like, according to God's perspective. The man began to question God about eternity. "How long is a million years?"

God answered the man, "a million years is a second."

"Wow," said the man, who then asked God, "How much is a million dollars?"

God answered, "A million dollars is a penny." The man pondered these two statements by God that a million years is a second and a million dollars is a penny. So the man asked God, "May I have a penny?"

God replied, "Wait a second."

God never says "wait a second" to the individual who believes on the finished work of Christ for salvation; He immediately imparts the free gift. In our last chapter John informed us about becoming a world-conqueror through faith. He now transitions to the topic of receiving eternal life through faith and the security that follows. Let's reverently read 1 John 5:6–13 together:

> This is He who came by water and blood—Jesus Christ; not only by water, but by water and blood. And it is the Spirit who bears witness, because the Spirit is truth. For there are three who bear witness in heaven: the Father, the Word, and the Holy Spirit; and these three are one. And there are three that bear witness on earth: the Spirit, the water, and the blood; and these three agree as one. If we receive the witness of men, the witness of God is greater; for this is the witness of God which He has testified of His Son. He who believes in the Son of God has the witness in himself; he who

does not believe God has made him a liar, because he has not believed the testimony that God has given of His Son. And this is the testimony: that God has given us eternal life, and this life is in His Son. He who has the Son has life; he who does not have the Son of God does not have life. These things I have written to you who believe in the name of the Son of God, that you may know that you have eternal life, and that you may *continue to* believe in the name of the Son of God (1 John 5:6–13).

This is the one who came by water and blood—Jesus Christ. He did not come by water only, but by water and blood. And it is the Spirit who testifies, because the Spirit is the truth. For there are three that testify: thea Spirit, the water and the blood; and the three are in agreement. We accept man's testimony, but God's testimony is greater because it is the testimony of God, which he has given about his Son. Anyone who believes in the Son of God has this testimony in his heart. Anyone who does not believe God has made him out to be a liar, because he has not believed the testimony God has given about his Son. And this is the testimony: God has given us eternal life, and this life is in his Son. He who has the Son has life; he who does not have the Son of God does not have life.

I write these things to you who believe in the name of the Son of God so that you may know that you have eternal life (1 John 5:6–13, NIV 84).

THE FAITH THAT SAVES AND SECURES—F

- What does it mean that Jesus "came by water and blood" in 1 John 5:6?
- Why does the NIV omit 1 John 5:7b-8a, as recorded in the NJKV?
- In 1 John 5:10, John penned, "He who believes in the Son of God has the witness in himself." What is "the witness" referred to there?
- How should 1 John 5:12 be viewed, in light of the Roman Catholic teaching on purgatory?

- How does John's purpose cited in 1 John 5:13 differ from his purpose in writing the Gospel of John according to John 20:30–31?

THE FAITH THAT SAVES AND SECURES—I

When I consider what many commentators have written about 1 John 5:6, "This is He who came by water and blood—Jesus Christ," I think of the following story: The instructor had just finished a lecture to the new paratroop recruits on the packing of a parachute. He ended with, "And remember, if it doesn't open, that's what is known as jumping to a conclusion!" I believe that many interpreters have jumped to the wrong conclusion concerning the meaning of the "water and blood" in 1 John 5:6.

Augustine linked "water and blood" to John 19:34, when Jesus' side was pierced and water and blood flowed from the wound. Calvin and Luther connected "water and blood" to the sacraments—communion and baptism. The common view today is for commentators to agree with Tertullian (AD 160?–240?) and see the water as referring to Jesus' baptism and the blood to his death via crucifixion. One thing all the above interpretations seemingly don't take into account is that John wrote in part to refute Docetism, which taught that Jesus only appeared to be a man. My conclusion about the "water and blood" is that Jesus was born in water, which shows that He literally was born and had a physical body, and that the blood clearly points to Jesus' death.

Let me share several other reasons why I've come, and hopefully not jumped, to my conclusion. One, Jesus told Nicodemus in John 3:5, "I say to you, unless one is born of water and the Spirit, he cannot enter the kingdom of God." In the very next verse, "water" is equated with "flesh." Jesus connected them in John 3:6, "That which is born of the flesh is flesh [first birth], and that which is born of the Spirit is spirit" [second or the heavenly birth]. The parallel idea in 1 John 5:6 ties "water" with physical birth.

Also, "water and blood" in 1 John 5:6 are joined by a preposition, which denotes the medium—with the meaning "by means of"—by which He came. That is, Jesus physically came "by means of water and blood." Finally, 1 John 5:5–6 are closely linked together. 1 John 5:5 shows that for someone to become an overcomer, he has to trust that Jesus, the historic person is the Son of God—and therefore, had to be born.

If the "water" speaks about Jesus' birth, then it would fit that the "blood" refers to His death. As the water and blood contradicted the teaching of Docetism (Jesus being a phantom), the blood further refuted the doctrine of Cerinthianism. Cerinthus taught that the divine Christ descended on the man Jesus at His baptism, but left Him before the crucifixion. John had demolished this notion by his eyewitness account that Jesus is both the Christ and the eternal Son of God.

Continuing in 1 John 5:6, John wrote, "And it is the Spirit who bears witness, because the Spirit is truth." Since "the Spirit is truth," He is to be believed concerning His testimony about Jesus as the Christ (1 John 5:1), and the Son of God (1 John 5:5). He, being God, cannot lie, and perpetually reveals truth.

The Word of God should be treated with the utmost respect. New Testament scholarship demands a careful scrutiny of all existing manuscripts to determine the original writings of John and every other book. The NKJV accurately begins 1 John 5:7 with, "For there are three who bear." It then continues until the first part of 1 John 5:8, "witness in heaven: the Father, the Word, and the Holy Spirit; and these three are one. And there are three that bear witness on earth." Sparse manuscript evidence exists for these words; they are generally prefaced with an asterisk, showing that they aren't found in the majority of Greek manuscripts or in the oldest manuscripts. Thus it is believed that all of those additional words are far removed from the time that John wrote his epistle. On account of these reasons, only the first six words of 1 John 5:7 should be considered authentic.

That said, the overwhelming manuscript evidence points to the first six words of 1 John 5:7 as original ("For there are three who bear") with the resumption of the biblical text in the middle of 1 John 5:8, "the Spirit, the water, and the blood; and these three agree as one." The three witnesses John cites (the Spirit, the water, and the blood) currently are testifying in full agreement, according to the present participle "bear," through the medium of the Word of God, that Jesus is the Christ.

According to Deuteronomy 19:15, there must be two or three human witnesses to find an accused person guilty of a crime. This is why John could write in 1 John 5:9, "If we receive the witness of men, the witness of God is greater; for this is the witness of God which He has testified of His Son." "If," which begins the sentence, is a first class condition assuming the statement to be true, which shows that we do receive man's testimony. John then argues from the lesser to the greater (an *a fortiori* argument): Since we accept man's testimony, how much more should we embrace God's?

Next, John writes, "He who believes in the Son of God has the witness in himself" (1 John 5:10). Not only does the child of God have the Bible as a testimony but also the internal witness of God's Spirit. Conversely, "he who does not believe God has made Him a liar, because he has not believed the testimony that God has given of His Son." Did you notice that no middle ground exists? Either you believe the multiple witnesses about Jesus, or you reject that multifaceted corroboration, and in essence call God a liar.

We have an innate witness through the Holy Spirit. How did this occur? "And this is the testimony: that God has given us eternal life, and this life is in His Son" (1 John 5:11). "Given" appears as an aorist and points to our salvation occurring in the past when we first believed, which is the means for our testimony of Jesus' sacrifice for us. Our "eternal life" speaks loudly because of our relationship with the Father, Son, and Holy Spirit.

John declares that all people belong in one of two camps, in 1 John 5:12: "He who has the Son has life; he who does not have the Son of God does not have life." The possessor of God's Son immediately and continually enjoys being born again. "Has" occurs twice in the first part of 1 John 5:12, and each time in the present tense. When you place faith in the Son, eternal life becomes a present possession. On the other hand, "he who does not have the Son of God does not have life." Again, the dual use of "has" in the present tense clarifies that the person who hasn't believed on Jesus doesn't habitually possess Him.

We now move on to the theme verse of 1 John: "These things I have written to you who believe in the name of the Son of God, that you may know that you have eternal life, and that you may *continue to* believe in the name of the Son of God" (1 John 5:13). John wrote his epistle to believers to assure them that once they depended upon Jesus as the Son of God, that they were eternally secure in Him. The word "that" directs us to the reason John wrote his epistle, "that you may know that you have eternal life." John desired his audience to understand that once they trusted in Jesus—the One who died for their sins and rose again—they were endowed with eternal life, and needed to continually rely upon the person and work of Jesus Christ.

John packs a lot into this paragraph; let's unpack it further under relationship.

THE FAITH THAT SAVES AND SECURES—R

I believe that a more expansive probing of John's theme would be helpful. He wrote, "These things I have written to you who believe in the name of the Son of God, that you may know that you have eternal life, and that you may *continue to* believe in the name of the Son of God" (1 John 5:13). Can someone lose his or her salvation once they've been saved? My goal will be to answer that question and leave you with an assurance of salvation.

For clarity purposes, when someone is saved they are eternally secure; the doctrine is called eternal security. Once a Christian understands this teaching, he or she has an assurance of salvation. God grants us eternal security; our comprehension of that truth produces the assurance.

Jesus gave a marvelous promise in John 10:28–29. He boldly stated, "And I give them eternal life, and they shall never perish; neither shall anyone snatch *them* out of My hand. My Father, who has given *them* to Me, is greater than all; and no one is able to snatch *them* out of My Father's hand." Earlier I referred to the strongest way in the Greek New Testament to show a definitive "no." It is called emphatic negation, and John penned Jesus' words using this double negative in John 10:28. The expression, "shall never" testifies that when Jesus grants "eternal life" that those who receive the gift "shall never perish." In other words, Jesus holds on to them forever.

A key thought to eternal security, as mentioned by Jesus in John 10:28–29, is that God holds on to us, and not we to Him. As a result of this understanding, Paul could write in Philippians 1:6, "being confident of this very thing, that He who has begun a good work in you will complete *it* until the day of Jesus Christ." Both the Father and Son have an eternal grip on us. Again using emphatic negation, Jesus shares, "All that the Father gives Me will come to Me, and the one who comes to Me I will by no means [emphatic negation here] cast out" (John 6:37). Don't worry about holding on to the Lord; *He's* got *you*.

What happens the moment that you are saved? Paul answers that question in Ephesians 1:13: "In Him [Jesus] you also *trusted*, after you heard the word of truth, the gospel of your salvation; in whom also, having believed, you were sealed with the Holy Spirit of promise." Upon believing in Jesus, God stamped His mark of ownership upon you by the Holy Spirit. The sealing ministry of the Holy Spirit declares that you are a genuine believer.

Did you notice that the seal above was with "the Holy Spirit of promise"? The Greek word "promise" is used today as with an engagement ring. When a fellow asks a girl to marry him, and she accepts, he places a band on her finger, which is a pledge that he will finish what he's promised. Just as the groom shows up on the wedding day to fulfill his word of honor, the Holy Spirit is God's down payment to us, that He will complete His guarantee, and that He'll bring us home to be with Him.

Can the seal of God's Holy Spirit upon us be broken? Stated otherwise, is it possible for God to violate His Word and leave us hanging at the altar without following through on His Word, which is His bond? Consider Ephesians 4:30: "And do not grieve the Holy Spirit of God, by whom you were sealed for the day of redemption." Once we are sealed, God cannot, and will not, violate His promise. My friend, you received God's seal upon believing; that seal cannot be broken, but will last unto Jesus' return on the day of redemption. Enjoy your security in Christ.

Now that we have a broadened understanding of John's teaching on eternal security, let's see how we are to apply this passage personally.

THE FAITH THAT SAVES AND SECURES—E

The apostle of love also had much to write about faith. Our two employment points will corroborate this. *Believe the evidence about Jesus' birth and death* is our first application point, derived from 1 John 5:6–9. There are levels of faith according to the Bible. Would I shake you to the core if I stated that even the demons believe the first employment point? Consider James 2:19: "You believe that there is one God. You do well. Even the demons believe—and tremble!" Although fallen angels haven't placed their faith in Jesus for salvation, they nonetheless know and believe "that there is one God." In the gospels, demons often recognized publicly who Jesus was—and trembled.

Why do I share this? Saving faith has two components. First, you must intellectually understand the gospel. The second part, concerning salvation, is that you must personally embrace the message of Jesus' substitutionary death and resurrection. John didn't want his readers to be shallow. He desired them to *believe the evidence about Jesus' birth and death*, to the degree that they would boldly proclaim that message to others based upon their faith. Furthermore, he wanted them to experience the inherent power in positionally being co-crucified with Christ, and manifest a new quality in their lives because Jesus conquered death and made His resurrection power available to them.

John desired to activate the believers' faith at Ephesus based upon Jesus' death and resurrection, and upon the multiple witnesses who testified to these historic truths. If you fully believe the evidence that John presented, then two results will occur. First, Galatians 2:20 will become a reality to you: "I have been crucified with Christ; it is no longer I who live, but Christ lives in me; and the *life* which I now live in the flesh I live by faith in the Son of God, who loved me and gave Himself for me." Employ the text by dying to self and living by faith in God's Son.

Two, your new life in Christ has placed you as positionally seated with Jesus in heavenly places, according to Ephesians 1:3 and 2:6. Paul also wrote about this, "Therefore we were buried with Him through baptism into death, that just as Christ was raised from the dead by the glory of the Father, even so we also should walk in newness of life" (Rom. 6:4). Positionally speaking, when Jesus died, so did you. Likewise, because He overcame death, you share in that liberating power. Employ the text by exhibiting your new quality of life through Jesus rising from the dead.

Our second employment point offers: *Know that belief in Jesus produces eternal life* (from 1 John 5:10–13). Let me ask you this searching question: What do you fear? Doesn't it make sense theologically that even if death can't separate us from God's presence, then we should attempt to accomplish whatever God calls us to do (even if we die in the process) because "to be absent from the body is to be present with the Lord" (2 Cor. 5:8)? We truly should be fearless as God's children.

Just the other day someone asked me, "Pastor, I know someone who recently took a mission trip to somewhere unsafe. Was that wise?" This made me think about my decisions to minister in El Salvador and Honduras. I knew that many local gang members have come to the DC area from El Salvador, which reveals the potential danger of that location, and that Honduras had the highest murder per capita rate in the world. Could I go and minister in places that were deemed less than safe? For me, the answer was a resounding yes.

I knew that God had led me to teach and preach in these locations. As a result of the divine guidance, I can still remember flying into San Pedro Sula, Honduras for the first time. God flooded me with peace and I *knew that belief in Jesus produces eternal life.* (Perhaps I'll share some of my hair-raising experiences in these locations in the future.) A deep belief in God's promises sets us free to minister without fear because of our eternal security. Embrace these two points, my friends, and your employment opportunities will increase.

CHAPTER NINETEEN

SIN WHICH BRINGS DEATH
1 JOHN 5:14–17

—≈∿≈—

One day Bill was hunting in the woods. It had been a slow day and he had yet to shoot any game. Suddenly, he heard a noise behind him. He whirled around and saw a ferocious mountain lion only twenty-five yards away. Bill quickly raised his rifle to his shoulder, took aim and pulled the trigger. Click. The rifle didn't fire.

Click…click…click. Again, nothing—the gun was malfunctioning. By this time, the mountain lion had started toward Bill.

In desperation, he threw down his rifle and ran. Faster and faster he ran, with the mountain lion chasing him. The faster Bill ran, the more the mountain lion gained on him. Finally, Bill came to the edge of a cliff. There was nowhere to go so he dropped to his knees and began to pray. "Oh Lord, I pray that you would turn this mountain lion into a Christian!"

As Bill looked up, he was surprised to see the mountain lion kneeling just a few feet away, praying, "Dear Lord, I pray that you'll bless this food that I'm about to partake to the nourishment of my body."

Prayer can be rather mysterious at times. Yet since 1 John 5:13 taught that the believer in Jesus Christ is eternally secure, 1 John 5:14–17 will show that we can have two immovable assurances in relation to prayer. Let's prayerfully and carefully read 1 John 5:14–17:

> Now this is the confidence that we have in Him, that if we ask anything according to His will, He hears us. And if we know that He hears us, whatever we ask, we know that we have the petitions that we have asked of Him.
>
> If anyone sees his brother sinning a sin *which does* not *lead* to death, he will ask, and He will give him life for those who commit

sin not *leading* to death. There is sin *leading* to death. I do not say that he should pray about that. All unrighteousness is sin, and there is sin not *leading* to death (1 John 5:14–17).

This is the confidence which we have before Him, that, if we ask anything according to His will, He hears us. And if we know that He hears us *in* whatever we ask, we know that we have the requests which we have asked from Him.

If anyone sees his brother committing a sin not *leading* to death, he shall ask and *God* will for him give life to those who commit sin not *leading* to death. There is a sin *leading* to death; I do not say that he should make request for this. All unrighteousness is sin, and there is a sin not *leading* to death (1 John 5:14–17, NASB).

THE PRAYERS FROM ETERNALLY SECURE SAINTS—F

- How do believers' know they are praying, "according to His will," as mentioned in 1 John 5:14?
- What does it mean that when we pray in light of God's will, "He hears us" in 1 John 5:14?
- How can we know what sins don't "lead to death" in 1 John 5:16?
- How can we know when someone *does* commit a sin "leading to death" in 1 John 5:16?
- Why shouldn't we pray about the sin "leading to death" in 1 John 5:16?

THE PRAYERS FROM ETERNALLY SECURE SAINTS—I

The saint's eternal security manufactures a holy boldness that enables him or her to courageously approach God's throne in prayer. John wrote, "Now this is the confidence that we have in Him, that if we ask anything according to His will, He hears us" (1 John 5:14). This is the fourth time that we've seen the word "confidence" in 1 John (2:28; 3:21; 4:17). Our freedom of speech is "in Him." Does "in Him" refer to the Father or the Son? Since our prayers are directly to the Father through the mediation of His Son, who sits at His right hand, it seems best to view the "in Him" pointing to the Father. Literally, the words "in Him" should be translated "toward Him" and orchestrate us to the Father.

We will examine the implications of the phrase "that if we ask anything according to His will" under relationship. For now, let it suffice to say that the child of God, who abides in Him, will be led by the indwelling Spirit to petition the Father for those things that He would be pleased to answer. Augustine expressed this concept well, "O Lord, grant that I may do Thy will as if it were my will; so that Thou mayest do my will as if it were Thy will." When John said concerning these prayers, "He hears us," he didn't mean just biologically, but that God answers prayers offered in conjunction with His divine plans.

The abiding Christian enjoys a liberty to communicate with God that leads to answered prayers, according to 1 John 5:15, "And if we know that He hears us, whatever we ask, we know that we have the petitions that we have asked of Him." The present tense verb "hears" shows that the Father regularly listens to our requests and responds based upon His perfect will and timing, whether now or later.

Continuing the topic of prayer, John writes in 1 John 5:16, "If anyone sees his brother sinning a sin *which does* not *lead* to death, he will ask, and He will give him life for those who commit sin not *leading* to death." How do you know if your Christian brother or sister has perpetrated a sin that causes God to discipline him or her, to the extent that He takes them home? The fact that he or she is still alive shows that the particular sin hasn't led to their demise yet.

There have been times when God has instantaneously struck someone with physical death for his or her sin. For instance, He did this with Aaron's oldest sons, Nadab and Abihu, in Leviticus 10, and Ananias and Sapphira in Acts 5. In both cases, the Lord deemed them worthy of instant judgment. When you observe a fellow Christian in disobedience to God, you should pray for God's mercy and that the breaker of His Word would repent. The singular Greek word translated "he will ask" refers to a person of inferior standing requesting something from a superior. It is used of a person to another person in Acts 3:2, and of an individual to God in John 14:13–14.

John then adds in 1 John 5:16b, "There is sin *leading* to death. I do not say that he should pray about that." The apostle uses a different verb for "pray" in the second half of this verse, this time it refers to one person asking another of equivalent standing. Jesus, who is eternally equal to the Father, used this word often when addressing His heavenly Father (John 14:16; 16:26; 17:9, 15, 20). The root meaning of this second usage of "pray" relates to questioning. John teaches that we shouldn't question the Father when He chooses to enact judgment upon a sinning brother or sister by bringing them immediately home to be with Him. It is appropriate to pray for an erring brother who is in sin, but once God decides to execute discipline, we are not to question His executive verdict because His will is perfect.

John culminates our paragraph with, "All unrighteousness is sin, and there is sin not *leading* to death" (1 John 5:17). Sin should never be taken lightly. In essence, all sin leads to death, but not all acts of disobedience bring about God's swift and final chastisement.

The Bible has much to say about prayer. Let's pursue this vast topic further.

THE PRAYERS FROM ETERNALLY SECURE SAINTS—R

Since the child of God has eternal security (1 John 5:13), he should display a firmness of conviction that the Father is for him and that He desires a vital relationship with him through prayer. Indeed, "Now this is the confidence that we have in Him," wrote John in 1 John 5:14, "that if we ask anything according to His will, He hears us." God is not a utilitarian genie who exists to capriciously honor our every whim; we must "ask . . . according to His will." What are the biblical truths we need to understand so that we can pray in alignment with God's desires?

First, we are not limited in what to pray for, as long as it meshes with the will of the Lord. Paul offers this insightful and encouraging truth in Ephesians 3:20, "Now to Him who is able to do exceedingly abundantly above all that we ask or think, according to the power that works in us." Let's be continually challenged to ask God for great things for His glory, being mindful of the angel's words to Mary in Luke 1:37, "For with God nothing will be impossible."

Next, please always remember, my dear brother or sister, that the goal in prayer is not to conform God to our desires but rather shape our will to His. James, the Lord's half-brother, corrected those who received his letter in James 4:3, "You ask and do not receive, because you ask amiss, that you may spend *it* on your pleasures." Their prayers were misguided because they were selfish. His recipients' self-serving hedonism is shown by the middle voice verb, which means asking for yourself, in the second occasion of "you ask" in James 4:3, and furthermore by James' accusation concerning fulfilling their own "pleasures."

Our Lord Jesus modeled the right spirit in prayer as He poured out His soul to the Father in Gethsemane. Just hours away from being scourged and crucified, He prayed, "Abba, Father, all things *are* possible for You. Take this cup away from Me; nevertheless, not what I will, but what You *will*" (Mark 14:36). When Jesus cried out, "not what I will," the "I will" is emphatic. He yielded His future to the Father's plans through agonizing prayer. We should do nothing less.

Another key aspect to consider about prayer is that God does not delight to answer the prayers of those in sin. Psalm 66:18 gives us helpful information on this: "If I regard iniquity in my heart, the Lord will not hear." The implication isn't that *literally* He doesn't hear us, but that He won't honor our requests because of unconfessed sin. Biblically speaking: For God to hear, is for Him to act. Observe how Jesus was "heard" concerning His resurrection from the dead when He poured out His heart to God in Hebrews 5:7, "who, in the days of His flesh, when He had offered up prayers and supplications, with vehement cries and tears to Him who was able to save from death, and was heard because of His godly fear." The Father didn't just listen to Jesus' prayers but responded to them by bringing Him back to life.

My treasured family member in Christ, we have a glorious privilege to approach God at any time through prayer. Let's honor the godly parameters that our heavenly Father has put down in His holy Word, and know that "this is the confidence that we have in Him, that if we ask anything according to His will, He hears us" (1 John 5:14).

It is now time for you to punch the time clock, and put these specific directives into practice.

THE PRAYERS FROM ETERNALLY SECURE SAINTS—E

I pray that the following two application points will help structure a prayer life for you that will be life-changing and add spiritual meat to your bones.

Be confident of answered prayer since you are eternally secure is our first employment point, derived from 1 John 5:14–15. A timid Christian doesn't foster a prayer life characterized by undaunted requests. Based upon Christ's preeminent priesthood (Heb. 4:14), His perfect person (Heb. 4:15), and His punctual provision (Heb. 4:16), the writer of Hebrews states, "Let us therefore come boldly to the throne of grace, that we may obtain mercy and find grace to help in time of need" (Heb. 4:16).

Once again, let's allow 1 John 5:14–15 to inspire us to cultivate a prayer life worthy of our secure calling. "Now this is the confidence that we have in Him, that if we ask anything according to His will, He hears us. And if we know that He hears us, whatever we ask, we know that we have the petitions that we have asked of Him."

Your first task is to pick the place where you will regularly pray. Dr. Luke shared this practice about Jesus in Luke 5:16, "So He Himself *often* withdrew into the wilderness and prayed." Find the right location for you. Make it your personal prayer closet, and know that the Father awaits your petitions.

Having a place to pray is important. Having a desire and a purpose in prayer is even more important, Therefore, I want you to start making a list with your prayer requests. This will not only remind you what to boldly ask on behalf of yourself and others, but you can visually enjoy writing down when God answers those intercessions, so that you may be encouraged to pray more often.

Our second employment point reminds us about the need to fervently pray for other saints. *Intercede for other believers since you are eternally secure* is our second application point, based upon 1 John 5:16–17. Your deliberate requests on behalf of a struggling brother or sister in Christ might just keep him or her alive. Prayer is powerful.

The Lord had a close relationship with Abraham. Before He destroyed the cities of Sodom and Gomorrah, He shared with his friend what He was about to do. Do you recall Abraham's response? He began to petition the Lord concerning the righteous believers who were enticed to live within those lurid places (Gen. 18:16–33). What difference did his intercession make? The Lord graciously rescued Lot and his daughters before destroying those places. Don't take your secure position in Christ lightly. You might just save a life.

Your second assignment is to pick a daily time or times to pray. Again, let Jesus be your guide. "Now in the morning, having risen a long while before daylight, He went out and departed to a solitary place; and there He prayed" (Mark 1:35). Also, I want you to make a list of struggling Christians that you know and begin to ask God to restore them to fellowship with Him.

Since you have your place and time(s) selected, along with your prayer list, exhibit your faith in God and live your Christian life courageously by *being confident of answered prayer* and *intercede for other believers*, because of your assurance of salvation.

CHAPTER TWENTY

THREE THINGS
JOHN WANTS US TO KNOW

1 JOHN 5:18–21

~~~⌇~~~

Four clergymen from the same town were talking one evening over coffee. The subject was their personal failings, and each agreed he had one. "That's right," the first said, "Take me, for instance. I like to hit the bottle every once in a while. I know my congregation doesn't know; however, I even preach against it from time to time. Yet somehow I can't resist a couple of shots to brace me now and then."

"Gambling is my snag," the second pastor admitted. "I do okay around here, but when I get out of town, I can't seem to resist. In fact, I lost a bundle on my last trip two weeks ago."

"Drinking and gambling don't cause me problems," the third said. "But I do cheat a bit on my income tax each year. It's tempting to keep quiet about some income I get on the side, but I figure I need the money. I know it's wrong, but I can't resist."

The fourth clergyman had been silent up to this point, so the others asked him what his greatest struggle was. "Well, I appreciate you fellows being so honest, so I guess I will be, too. Drinking and gambling have never appealed to me and I don't cheat on my income tax, but I do have one serious vice: I just love to gossip, and right now I can hardly wait to leave here."

Clergyman number four wanted to exit the premises immediately so he could tell everyone about the vices of the first three men. He thought there were three things everyone should know. John also wanted the saints to know three things from 1 John 5:18–21; he imparts a triad of assurances to the brethren as he closes his letter. Let's read them thoughtfully:

We know that no one who is born of God sins; but He who was born of God keeps him, and the evil one does not touch him. We know that we are of God, and that the whole world lies in *the power of* the evil one. And we know that the Son of God has come, and has given us understanding so that we may know Him who is true; and we are in Him who is true, in His Son Jesus Christ. This is the true God and eternal life.

Little children, guard yourselves from idols (1 John 5:18–21).

We know that everyone fathered by God does not sin, but God protects the one he has fathered, and the evil one cannot touch him. We know that we are from God, and the whole world lies in the power of the evil one. And we know that the Son of God has come and has given us insight to know him who is true, and we are in him who is true, in his Son Jesus Christ. This one is the true God and eternal life. Little children, guard yourselves from idols (1 John 5:18–21, NET).

JOHN'S CLOSING TRIO OF ASSURANCES—F

- How literally should we take the English translation that states, "We know that whoever is born of God does not sin" in 1 John 5:18?
- What does John mean by "he who has been born of God keeps himself" in 1 John 5:18?
- How literally should we take John when he wrote, "and the whole world lies *under the sway of* the wicked one" in 1 John 5:19?
- What is the "understanding" that Jesus has given us, as mentioned in 1 John 5:20?
- Does John refer to the Father or Son when he writes, "This is the true God and eternal life" in 1 John 5:20?
- What are the "idols" that the children of God are to stay away from in 1 John 5:21?

JOHN'S CLOSING TRIO OF ASSURANCES—I

"We know" gives us John's beginning to our first three verses. This Greek word for "know" doesn't mean experiential knowledge this time, but denotes perceiving, or to know intuitively. Christians instinctively know certain things when they have believed on Jesus for salvation.

"We know that whoever is born of God does not sin" according to the apostle in 1 John 5:18. The passive voice for "born of God" shows that this is a work of God; He's the One who moved upon us to be saved by embedding the Holy Spirit within us. John uses the present tense verb for "sin" in the expression "does not sin" and testifies to the fact that the Lord's born-again saints cannot live a life of sin.

How does the child of God not sin? John adds in, "but he who has been born of God keeps himself and the wicked one does not touch him" (1 John 5:18). Again the apostle uses a present tense verb ("keeps") to demonstrate the believer's regularity of protecting himself from sin. John's point was that when the believer guards his life from participating in sin, Satan can't "touch" or affix himself to the saint. We need to have a closed-door policy when it comes to sin, which will keep Satan on the outside looking in.

The second "we know" statement appears in 1 John 5:19, "We know that we are of God, and the whole world lies *under the sway of* the wicked one." John restates the theme of 1 John (from 5:13) "that we are of God." Eternally we are fastened to Jesus. Yet "the whole world lies *under the sway of* the wicked one." "The whole world" here refers to the unsaved world. All believers belong to God, while all non-believers unwittingly are under the power or control of the devil. For John, there exists no in between or middle ground; you either belong to God or Satan.

Moving to our third consecutive concept of knowledge by perception, John wrote, "And we know that the Son of God has come and has given us an understanding" (1 John 5:20). The Greek word for "understanding" speaks of an ability to know the truth. John continues, "that we may know Him who is true, in His Son Jesus Christ." This time, the apostle of love writes of experiential knowledge, via the singular Greek word translated "we may know," and points to the base of our knowledge coming through Jesus, who is true.

John then makes a revealing assertion to close out 1 John 5:20: "This is the true God and eternal life." Does the referent for "this" direct us back to the Father or Son? Let me give you four reasons why I believe Jesus is "the true God and eternal life." He is the nearest antecedent—called "His Son Jesus" in the same verse. Two, Jesus is called "the life" in John 11:25 and 14:6, and here the One who gives "eternal life." The third argument is that He is called "true" five times by John in the apostle's writings ("true light" in John 1:9 and 1 John 2:8; "true bread" in John 6:32; "true vine" in John 15:1; and "true witness" in Revelation 3:14).

The fourth reason is that of a Christological inclusion. In other words, 1 John 1:1–2 (the beginning of our epistle) points to Jesus being God, and 1 John 5:20 (the end of our letter) shows Him to be the same. Like bookends, this epistle begins and ends with Jesus being proclaimed as God. John did the same thing in his gospel (see John 1:1; 20:28). Hence, Jesus "is the true God and eternal life," according to John.

John's final command occurs in 1 John 5:21, "Little children, keep yourselves from idols. Amen." Based upon the recipients' perceived knowledge (1 John 5:18–20), they are to protect themselves from anything that would replace the true God. Although some commentators view the idolatry in a figurative or non-literal sense here, it seems best to take John to be referring to literal idols. After all, the Ephesians had an attachment to literal idols when Paul proclaimed Christ to them and they were set free (see Acts 19:23–41). Today, many people around the world worship idols, and children of God can also do the same figuratively by not guarding their hearts from anything that would sit on its throne and rule.

JOHN'S CLOSING TRIO OF ASSURANCES—R

A good spiritual shepherd tends to his flock and encourages the sheep not to sin. John earlier emphasized this message. In 1 John 2:1 he wrote, "My little children, these things I write to you, that you may not sin. And if anyone sins, we have an Advocate with the Father, Jesus Christ the righteous."

Subsequently in 1 John 3:9, John taught that believers couldn't sin habitually, "Whoever has been born of God does not sin, for His seed remains in him; and he cannot sin." John gives us more biblical dots to connect in his epistle when he writes, "We know that whoever is born of God does not sin; but he who has been born of God keeps himself, and the wicked one does not touch him" (1 John 5:18). I believe it would be beneficial to trace this thought beyond John's writings.

The reason that God's children cannot have an unbroken pattern of sin is because of their new nature. When the saint is armed with the knowledge of his biblical position in Christ, he can apply that freeing information and regularly experience victory over the old man. Paul taught, "Therefore, if anyone is in Christ, he is a new creation; old things have passed away; behold, all things have become new" (2 Cor. 5:17). The moment you were born again, God gave you a new capacity, through the empowerment of God's implanted Spirit to thwart the attacks of Satan (who appeals to his ally in our fallen nature) and enjoy a sustained triumph.

John keenly declares that "he who has been born of God keeps himself." The key to guarding yourself from sin derives from our eternally secure position in the Father and Son, who protected Jesus' disciples. The Greek word "keeps" appears in John 17:11 of the Father, and then of the Son in John 17:12. Observe Jesus' prayer in John 17:11–12, "Now I am no longer in the world, but these [Jesus' disciples] are in the world, and I come to You. Holy Father, keep through Your name those whom You have given Me, that they may be one as We are. While I was with them in the world, I kept them in Your name. Those whom You gave Me I have kept; and none of them is lost except the son of perdition [Judas], that the Scripture might be fulfilled."

The doctrine of sanctification—which would be hampered if believers weren't eternally secure—consists of the process of God whereby the Holy Spirit is conforming us to the image of Jesus Christ. There are three parts in the process. First is our position, which I'll address shortly. Next comes the day-by-day incremental change described by progressive sanctification (2 Cor. 3:18). Lastly, the New Testament describes our pending sanctification. First John 3:2 instructs us that when Jesus returns we'll be fully conformed to His likeness.

Let's return to the doctrine of positional sanctification. In essence, when Jesus died, we died with Him. Paul elaborated upon this in Galatians 2:20, "I have been crucified with Christ; it is no longer I who live, but Christ lives in me; and the *life* which I now live in the flesh I live by faith in the Son of God, who loved me and gave Himself for me." Let me pose this question to you. How do dead people respond to temptation? The obvious answer is: They don't. Since we have been co-crucified with Jesus positionally, our new capacity enables us to be dead to sin and not yield to the cravings of the flesh.

George Muller accomplished great things for God in England in the nineteenth century. His burden consisted of founding orphanages and trusting the Father solely to supply all the needs through the vehicle of prayer. As Muller put it, "There was a day when I died. Died utterly; died to George Muller, his opinions, preferences, tastes, and will—died to the world, its approval or censure—died to the approval or blame even of my brethren or friends—and since then I have studied only to show myself approved unto God." Ponder long and hard what this mighty man of God applied to his life based upon his positional sanctification, which moved the Almighty to regularly answer his prayers so that he accomplished incredible things for God's glory.

Not only are we to put the deeds of the flesh to death through our co-crucifixion with Christ positionally; we are also to exemplify our new capacity to live victoriously on account of Jesus' resurrection. Speaking about our God-given ability not to submit to sin and live righteously through the raising of our Lord from the dead, Paul writes in Romans 6:4, "that just as Christ was raised from the dead by the glory of the Father, even so we also should walk in newness of life."

My friend, employing your position in Christ allows you to not be touched by the wicked one, according to the last part of 1 John 5:18: "and the wicked one does not touch him." There is a ground game being fought between you and the powers of darkness. Paul addressed this topic in Ephesians 4:26–27 when he wrote, "Be angry, and do not sin, do not let the sun go down on your wrath, nor give place ["ground"] to the devil." Applying what John taught in 1 John 5:18 prevents Satan from having unnecessary access to your life. Implement being co-crucified and resurrected with Jesus, and God will cause you to flourish spiritually.

JOHN'S CLOSING TRIO OF ASSURANCES—E

As the clergyman at the beginning of our chapter couldn't wait to share three things about his friends, John equally had three assurances that he wanted to impart to his congregation. *Be assured of victory over sin* gives us our first employment point, from 1 John 5:18. Biblically speaking, knowledge is power; however, you have to choose to apply what you've learned. First John 5:18 says, "We know that whoever is born of God does not sin; but he who has been born of God keeps himself, and the wicked one does not touch him."

Abiding in Christ is a key component to sustaining victory in the Christian life. We have an obligation to be resolved to walk with God and not capitulate to sin. Paul informed his younger colleague Timothy in 2 Timothy 2:19, "Nevertheless the solid foundation of God stands, having this seal: The Lord knows those who are His, and let everyone who names the name of Christ depart from iniquity." The triumphant Christian life isn't lived on cruise control. Obediently commit right now, my brother or sister, to experience a life of victory by guarding yourself from sin and by not allowing the wicked one to infiltrate your life.

This leads nicely to our second application point: *Be assured of victory over Satan,* from 1 John 5:19. Although the Prince of Darkness might be in control over all the earth's unsaved population, he doesn't preside over you. John writes, "We know that we are of God, and the whole world lies *under the sway of* the wicked one." When Satan comes to allure you to compromise your Christian convictions, remind him that you are already a world-conqueror in Christ.

Please don't permit your guard to drop, because Satan still seeks to ruin your Christian testimony. Peter reminds the saints, "Be sober, be vigilant; because your adversary the devil walks about like a roaring lion, seeking whom he may devour. Resist him, steadfast in the faith, knowing that the same sufferings are experienced by your brotherhood in the world" (1 Pet.

5:8–9). Right now, bow your head and tell the Lord that you will fight from victory and "resist him, steadfast in the faith."

I can't think of a better point to wrap up our time together than the third employment point, *Be assured of eternal life through Jesus the true God*, which derives from 1 John 5:20–21. Be assured, my precious brother and sister in Christ: You aren't holding on to God and Jesus, but they are holding on to you. Please memorize John 10:28–29, and joyfully carry about the assurance of your salvation daily: "And I [Jesus] give them eternal life, and they shall never perish; neither shall anyone snatch them out of My hand. My Father, who has given *them* to Me, is greater than all; and no one is able to snatch *them* out of My Father's hand."

ALSO AVAILABLE FROM

KEN J. BURGE, SR.

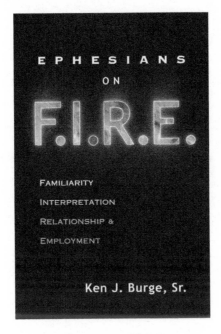

Ephesians on F.I.R.E.
ISBN: 9781940269412

and Coming in 2016
Revelation on F.I.R.E.

CPSIA information can be obtained at www.ICGtesting.com
Printed in the USA
BVOW08s1844231215

430919BV00001B/2/P